Snakes in Hats

2024 Artwork by
Keilani McConnell

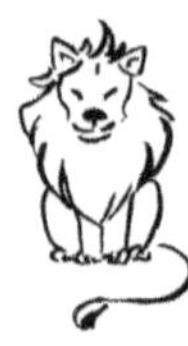

First published by Spirit Lion, an imprint of Nine Lions, 2025

Copyright © 2025 Keilani McConnell

All rights reserved. No part of this book may be used or reproduced in any manner without the prior written permission of the copyright owner.

No generative artificial intelligence (AI) was used in the creation of this work. The creator expressly prohibits any entity from using this publication to train AI technologies to generate artwork or text, including, without limitation, technologies capable of generating works in the same style or genre as this publication. The creator reserves all rights to license uses of this work for generative AI training and development of machine learning models.

Paperback ISBN: 978-1-963482-06-5

All artwork by Keilani McConnell, drawn traditionally using different mediums, including watercolor, markers, pencil, and inking pens on cold-press and hot-press watercolor paper, and marker paper.

Text set in Overlock

keilanimcconnellart.com

Flower Fairies

Azalea

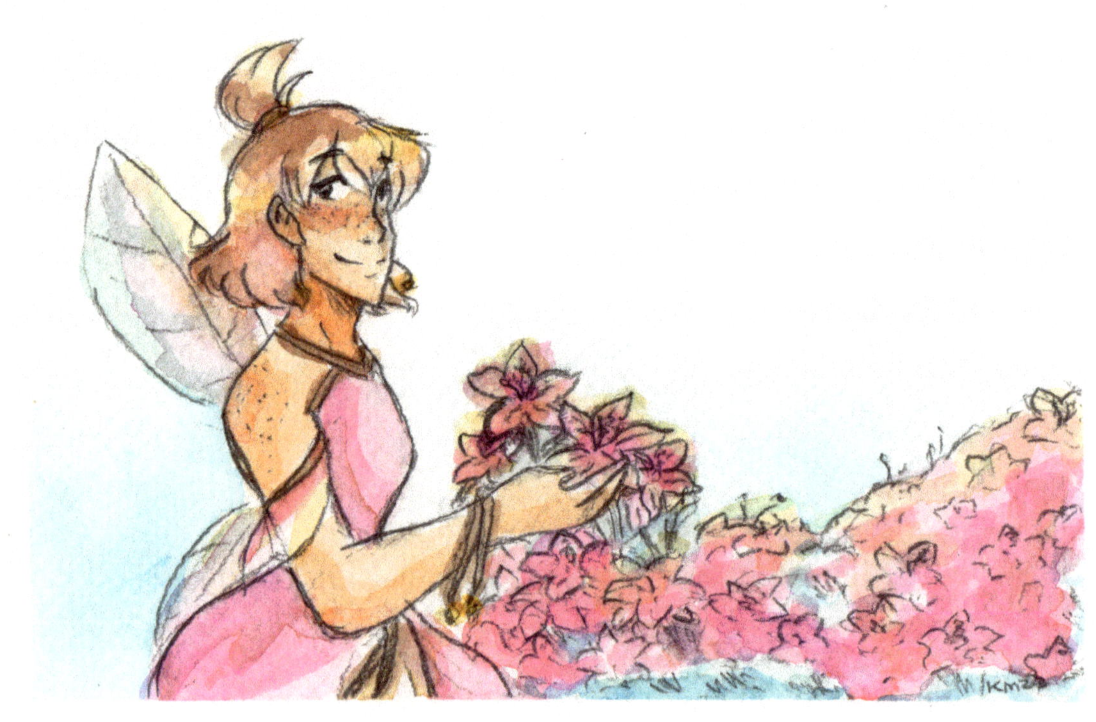

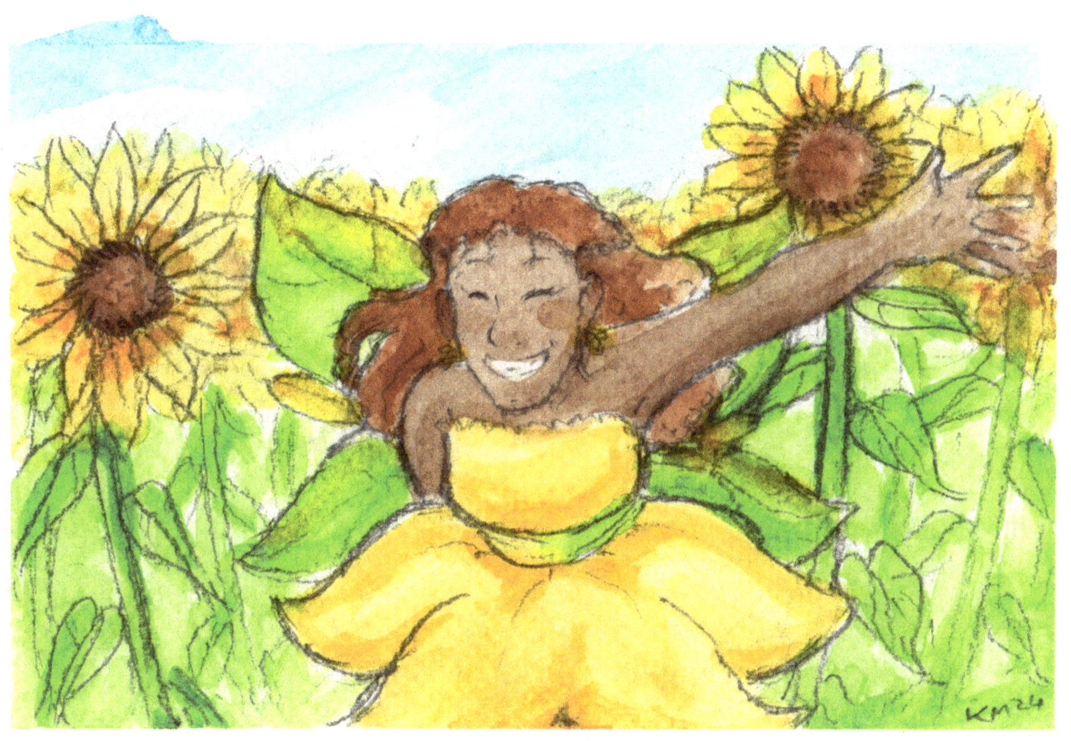

Lily

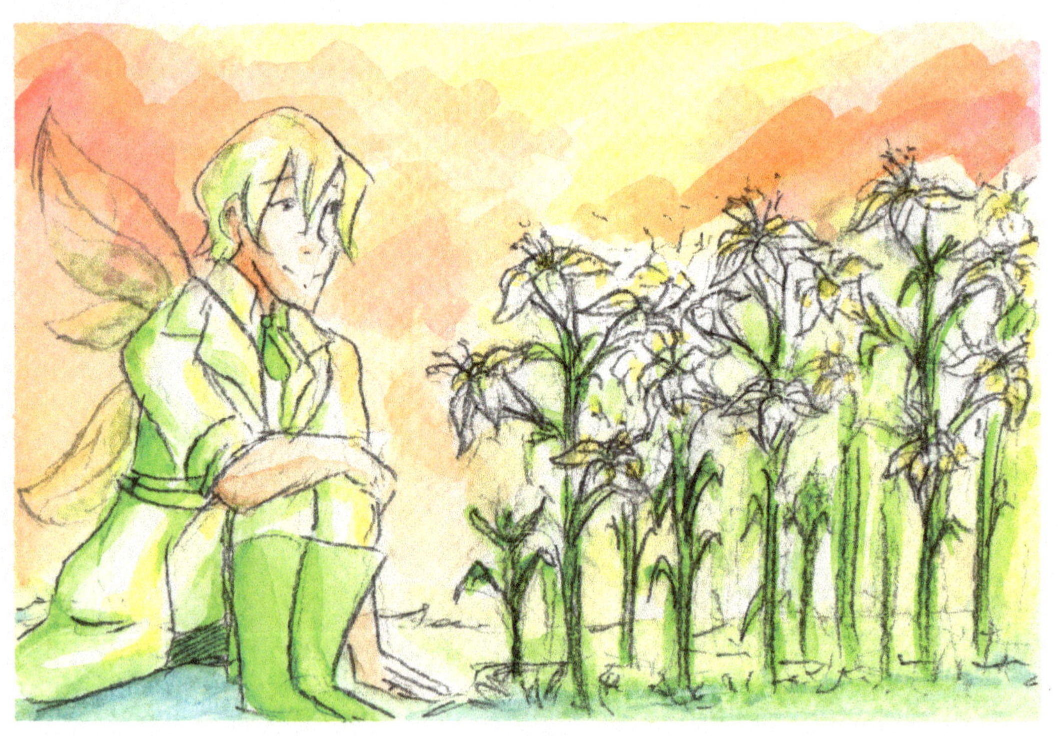

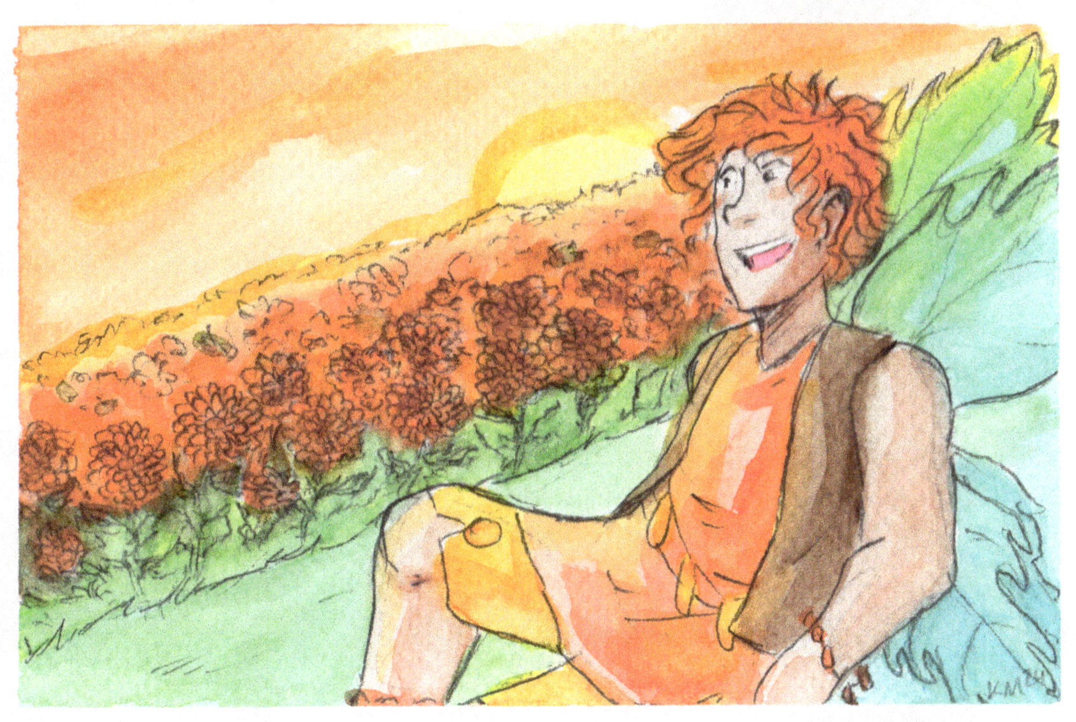

Daisy

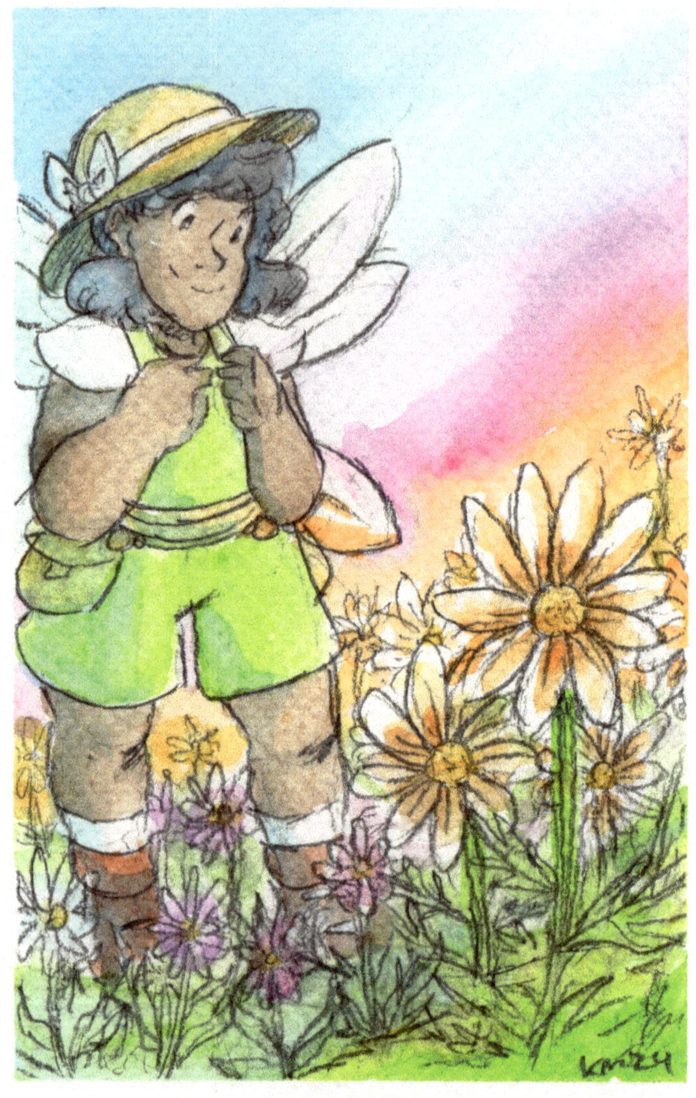

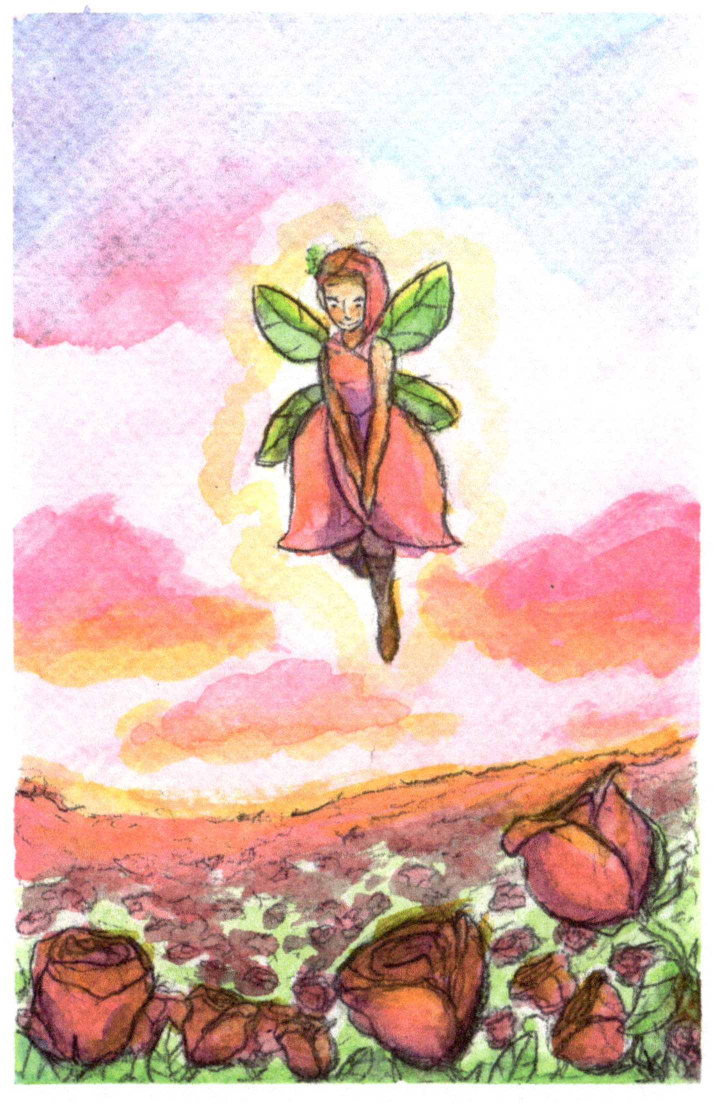

Night-scented
Stock

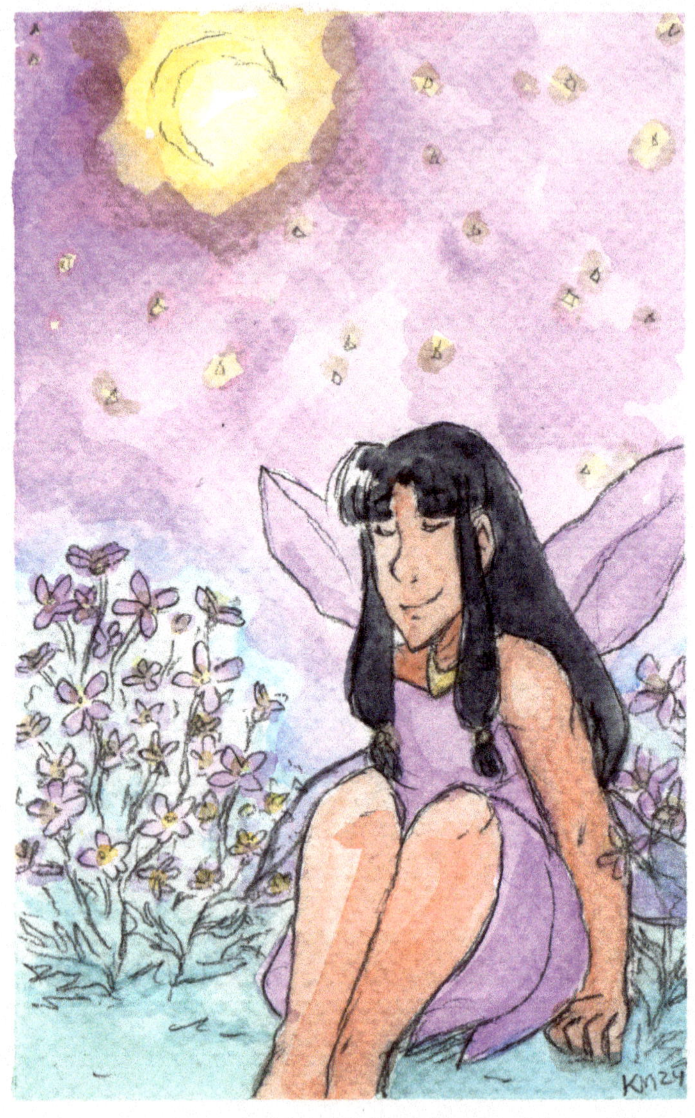

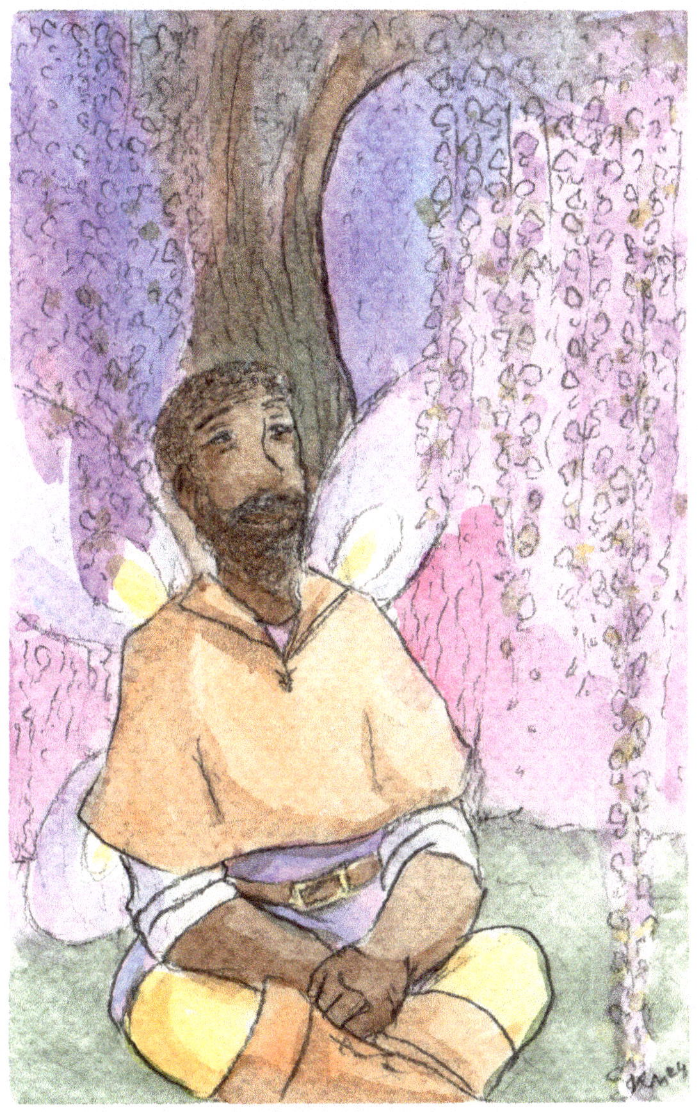

Japanese
Wisteria

Weather
Dogs

Stormy Great Dane

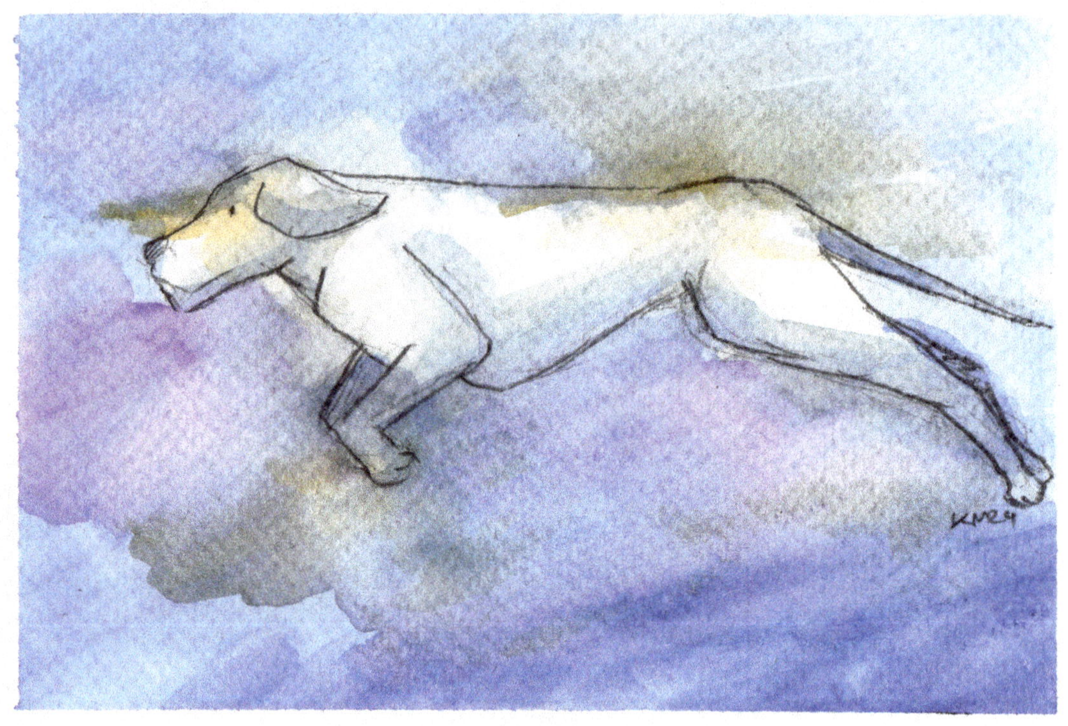

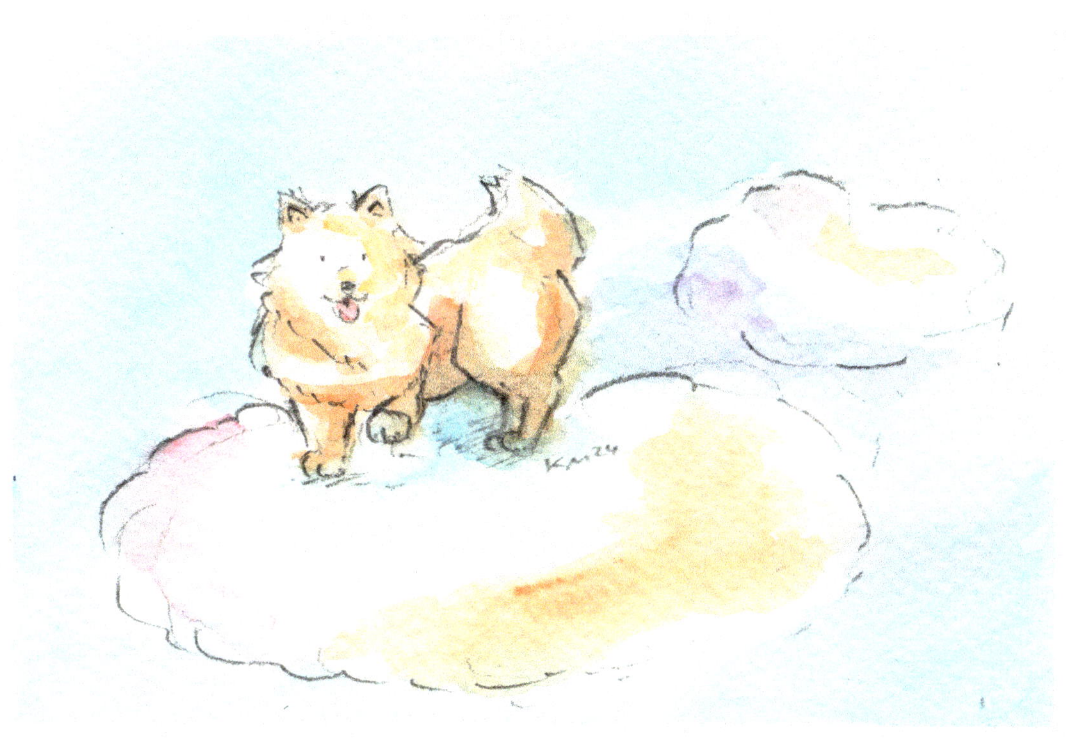

Snowy
Golden
Retriever

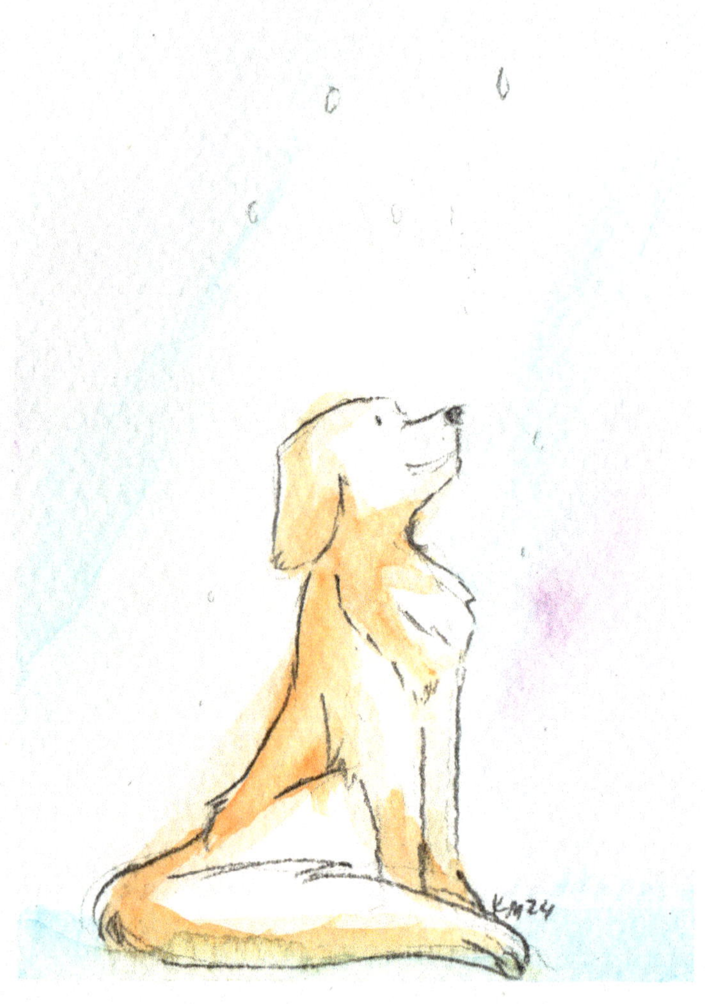

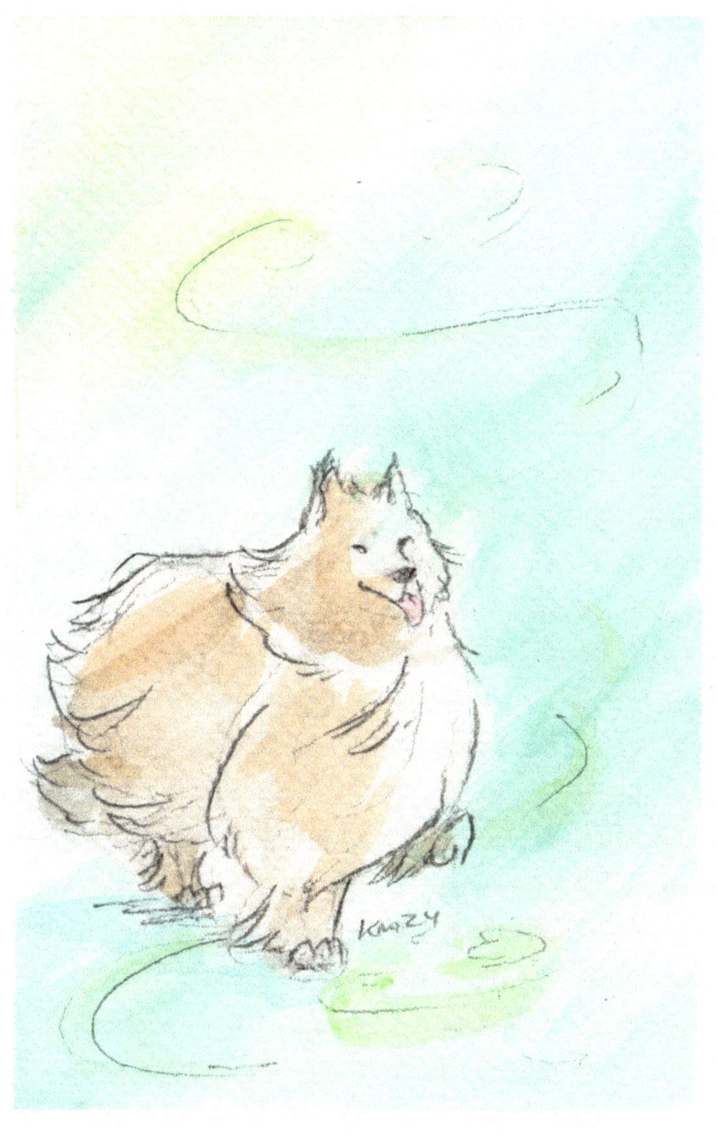

Sunny Chihuahua

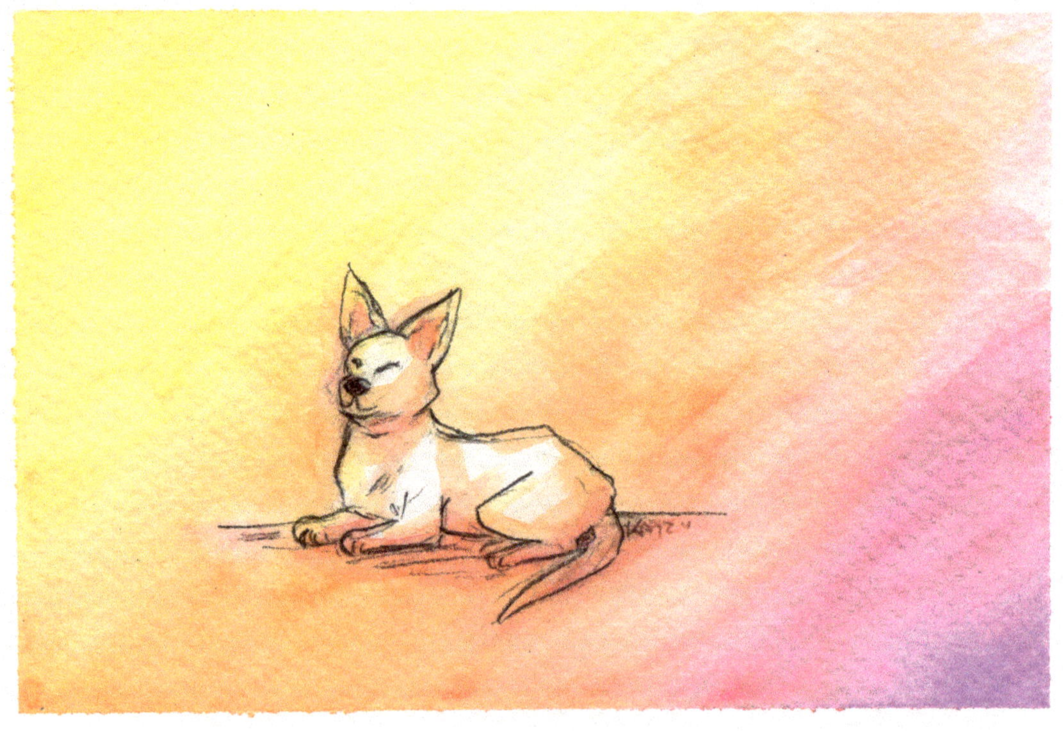

Dalmatian in the Rain

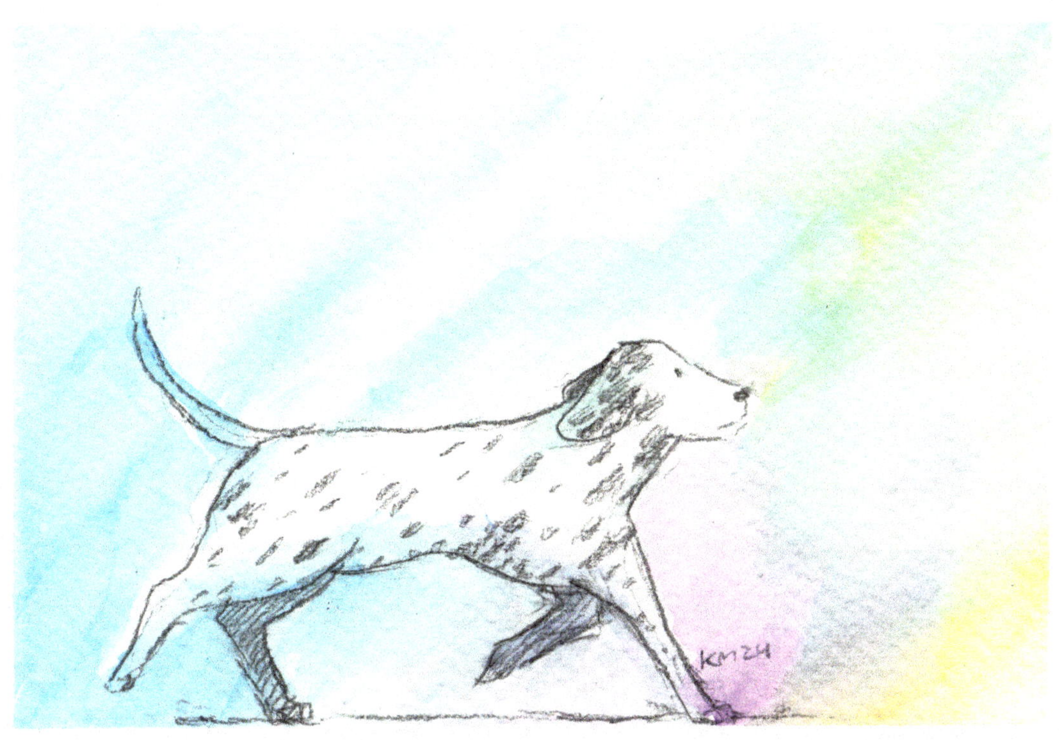

Crystal Explorers

Pink

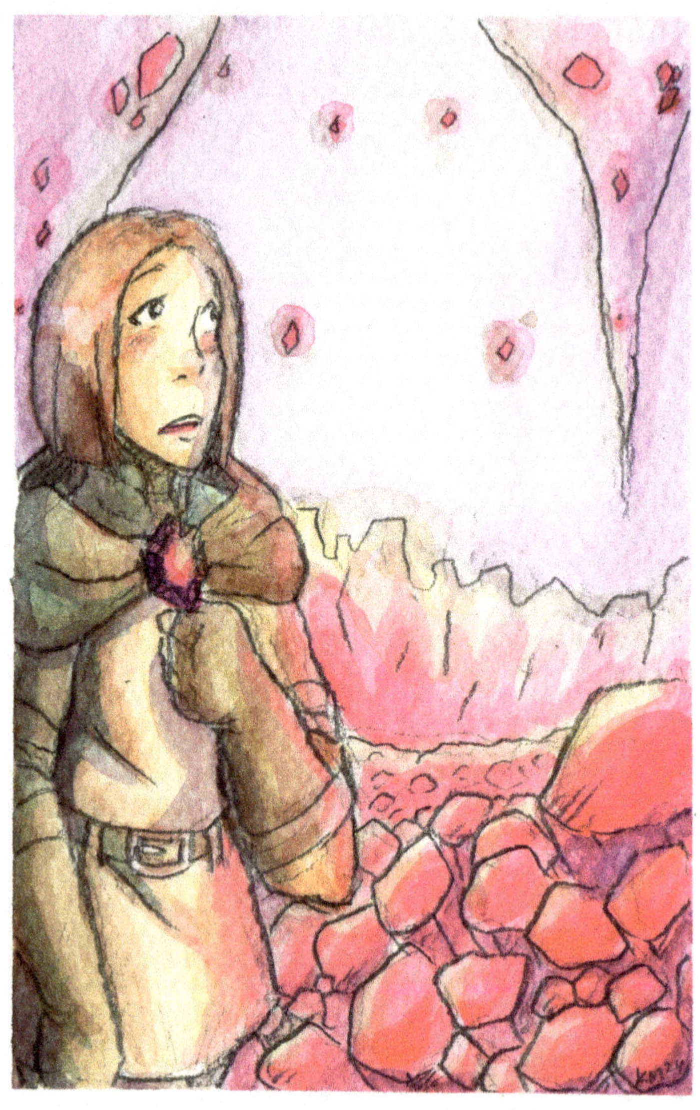

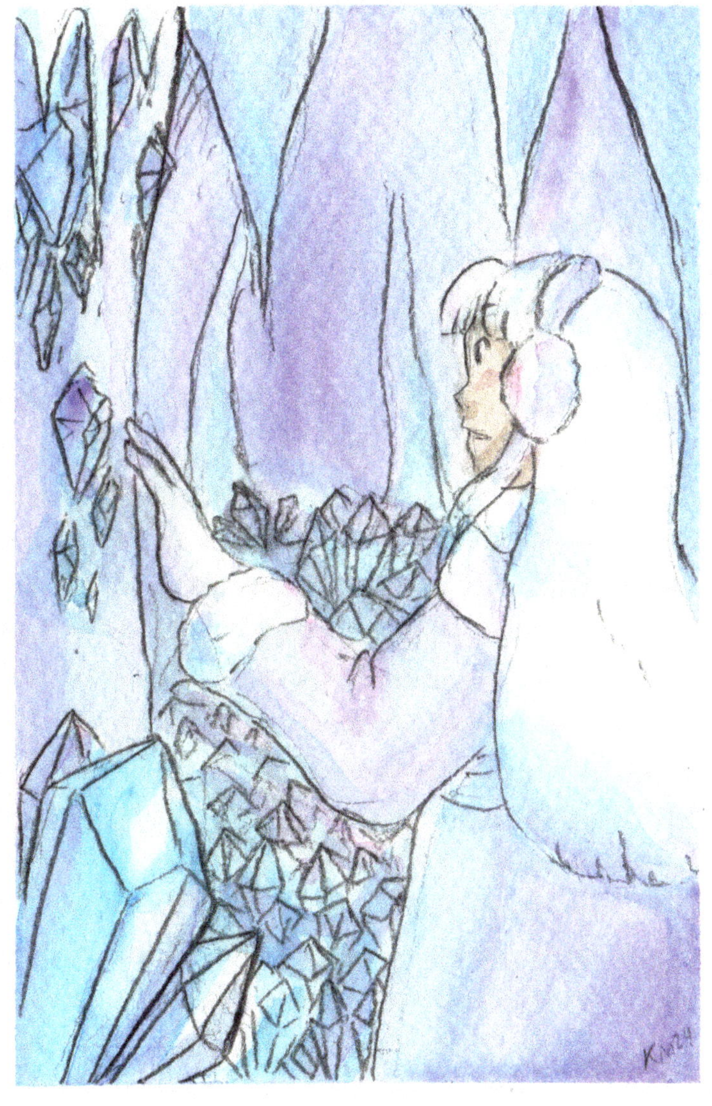

Green

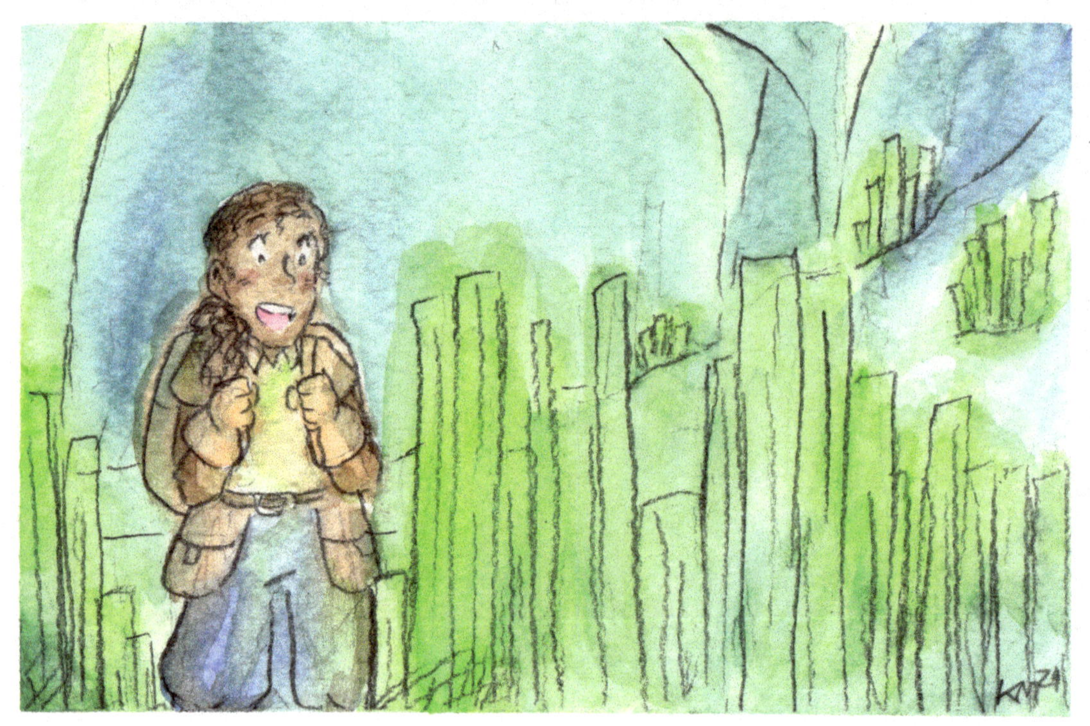

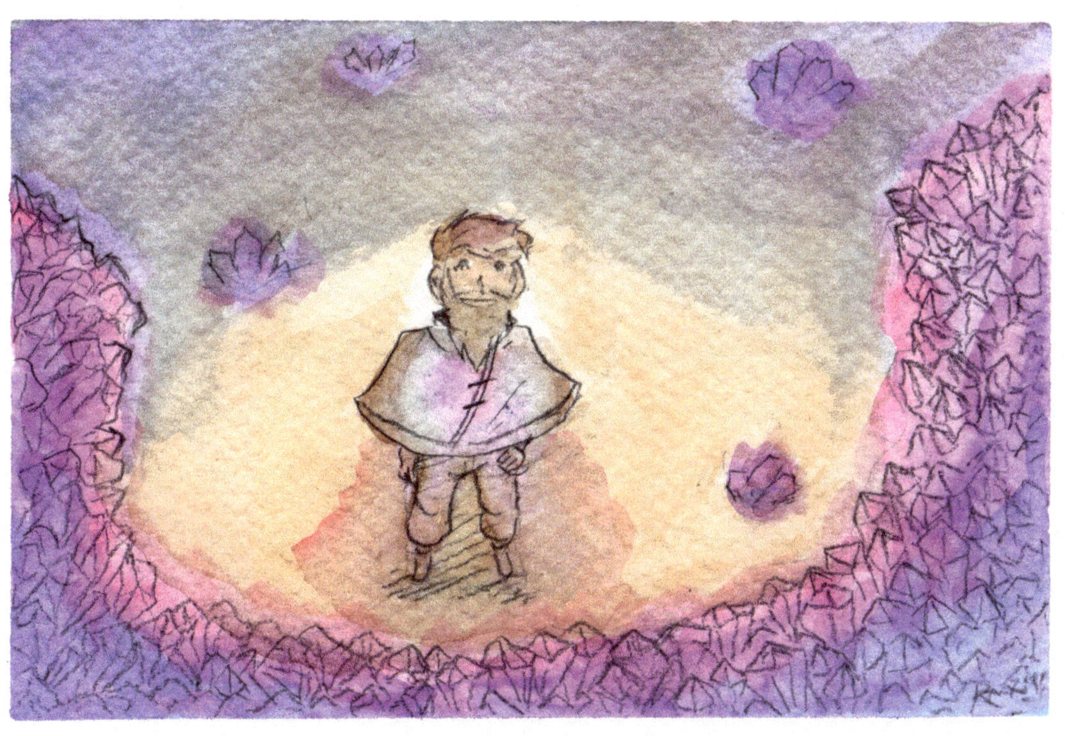

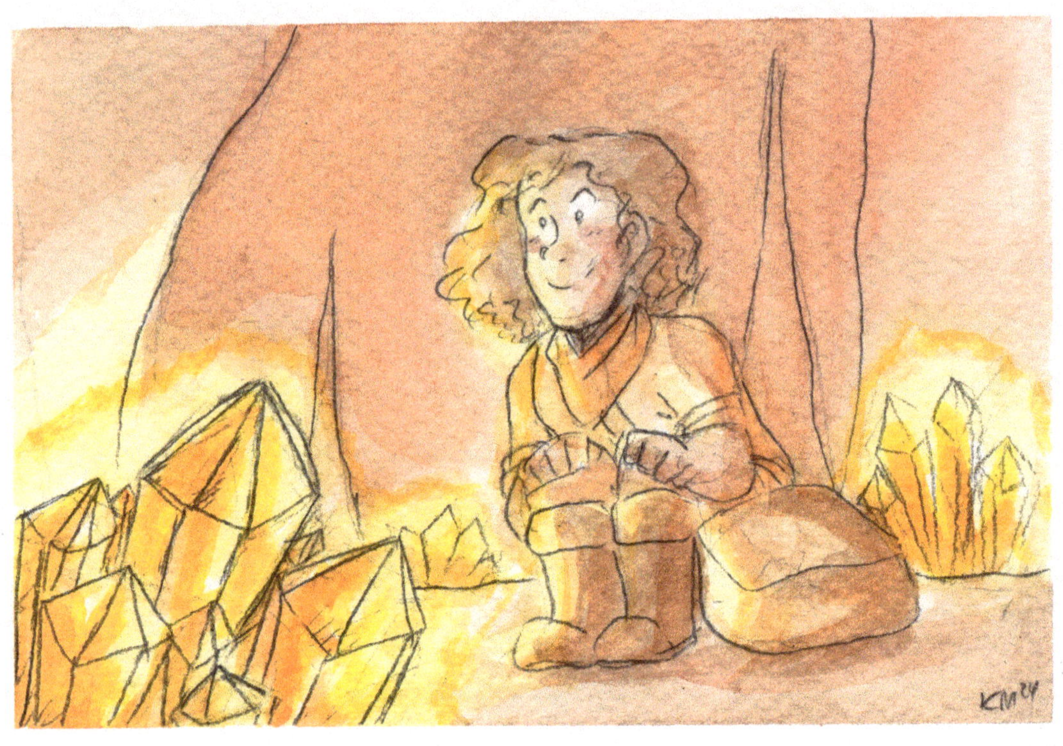

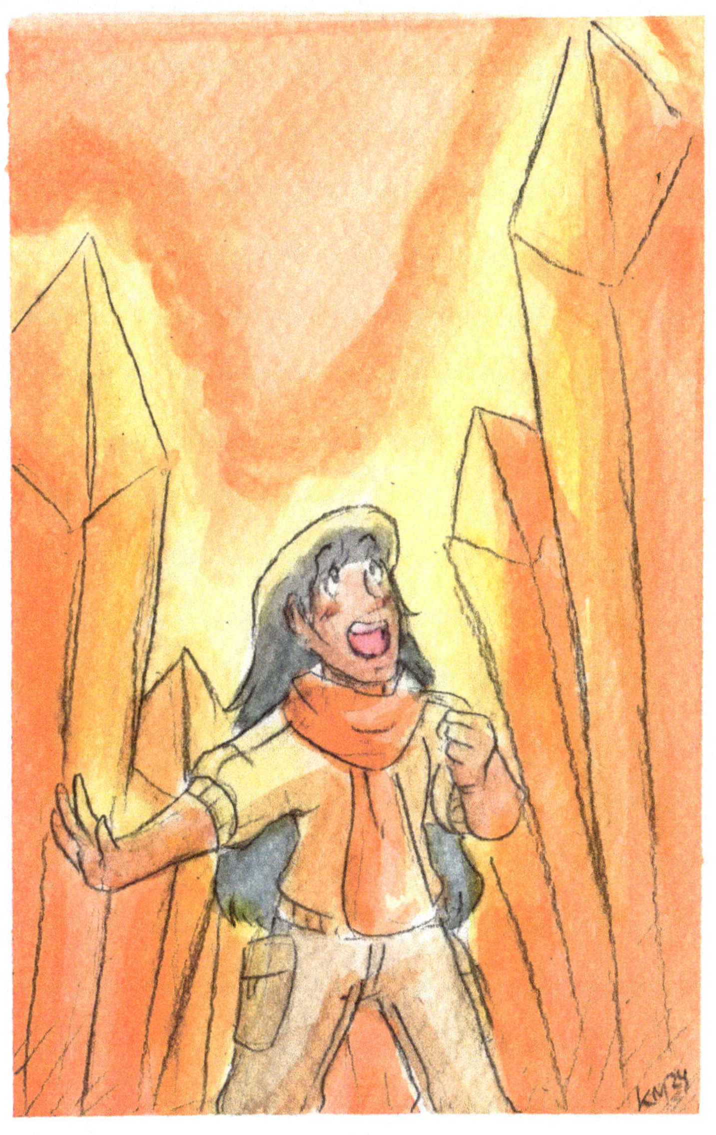

Rainbow

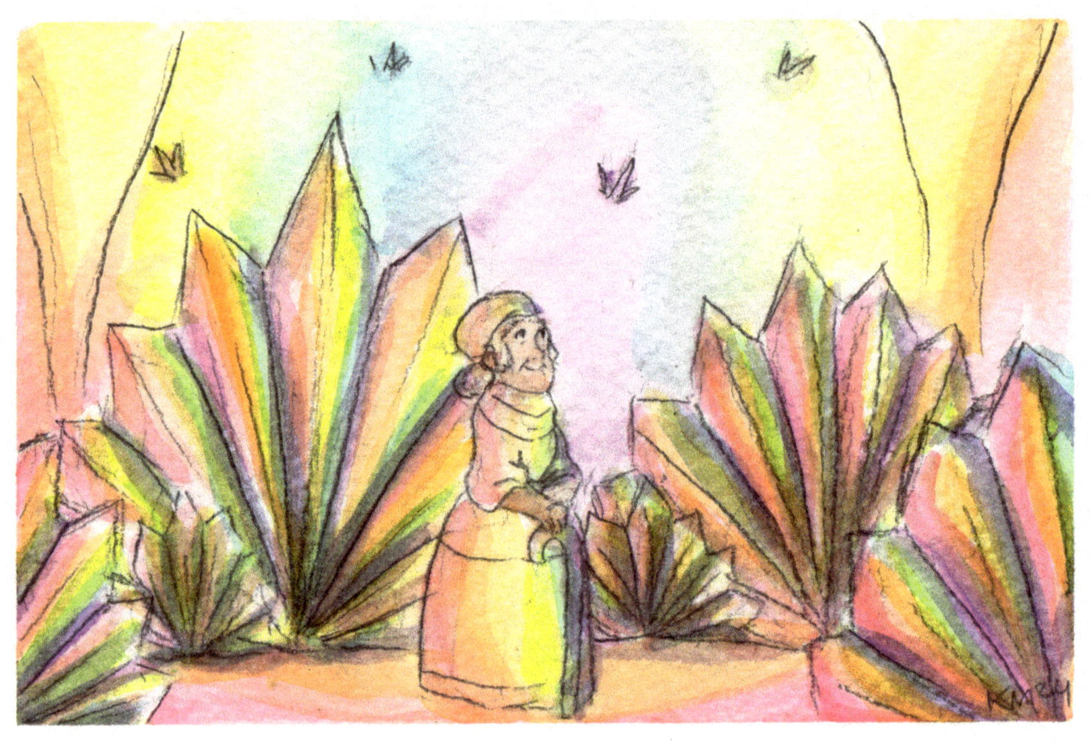

Dino
Desserts

T-Rex Ice
Cream Cone

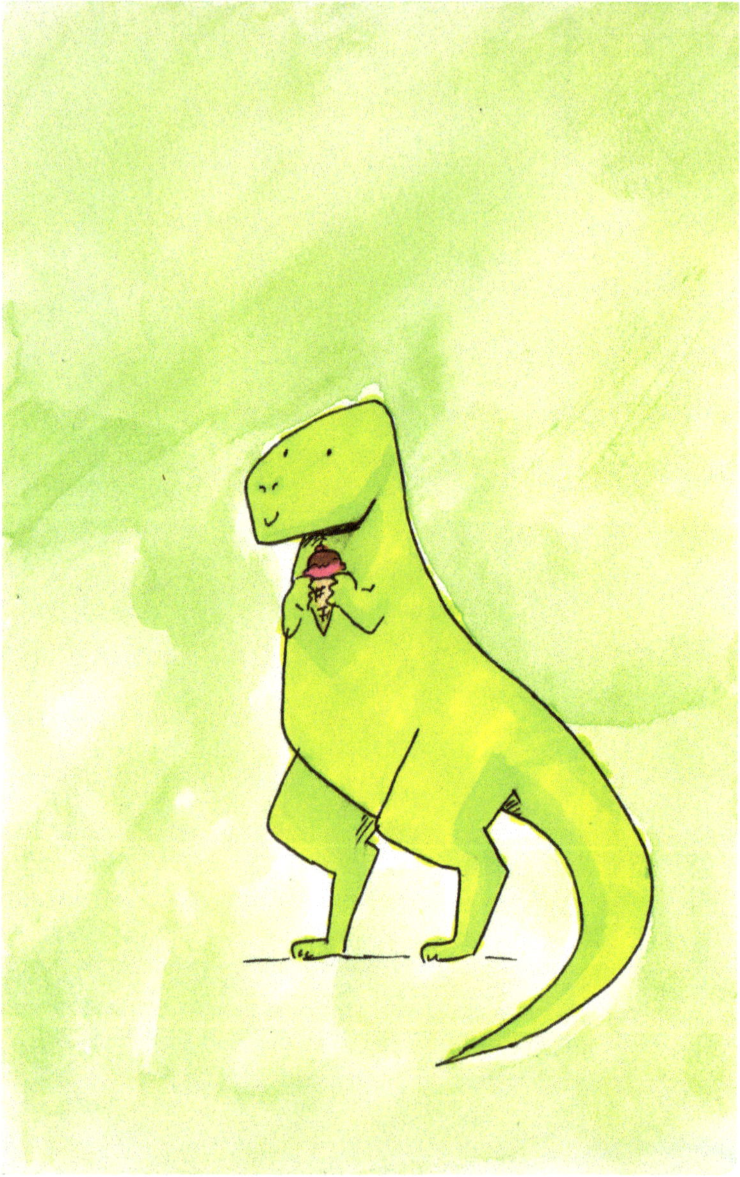

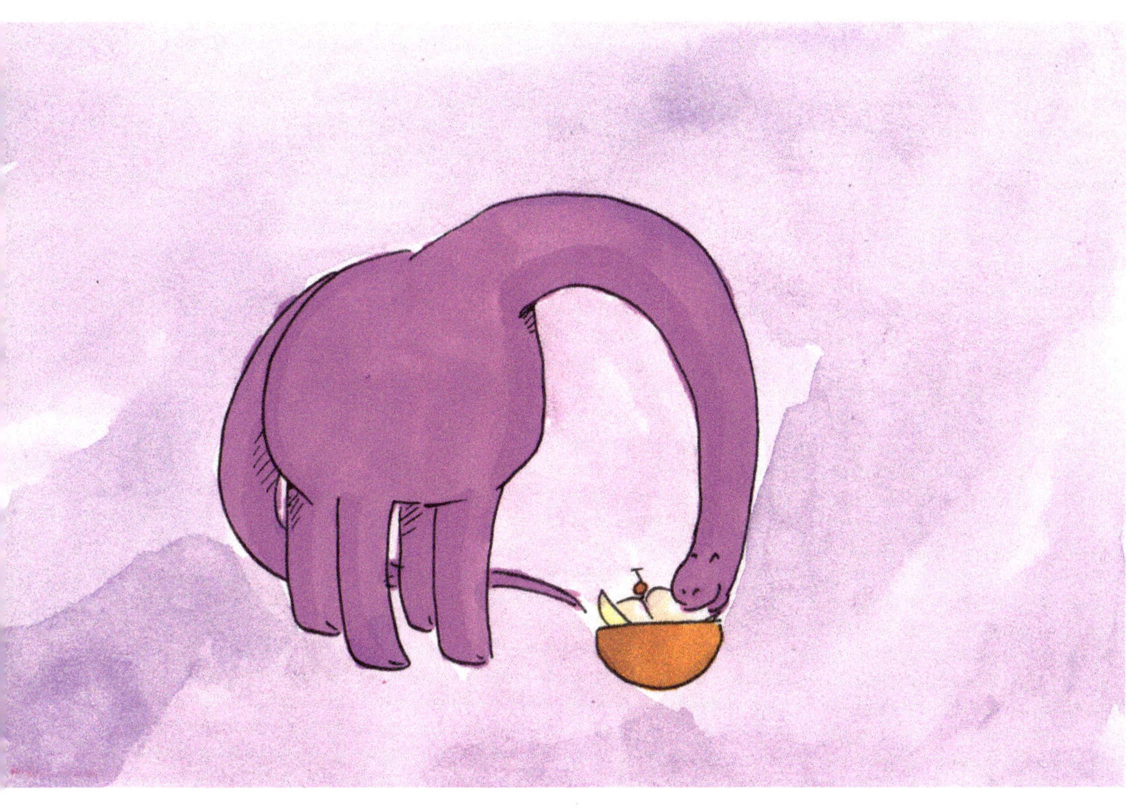

Stegosaurus Cookie

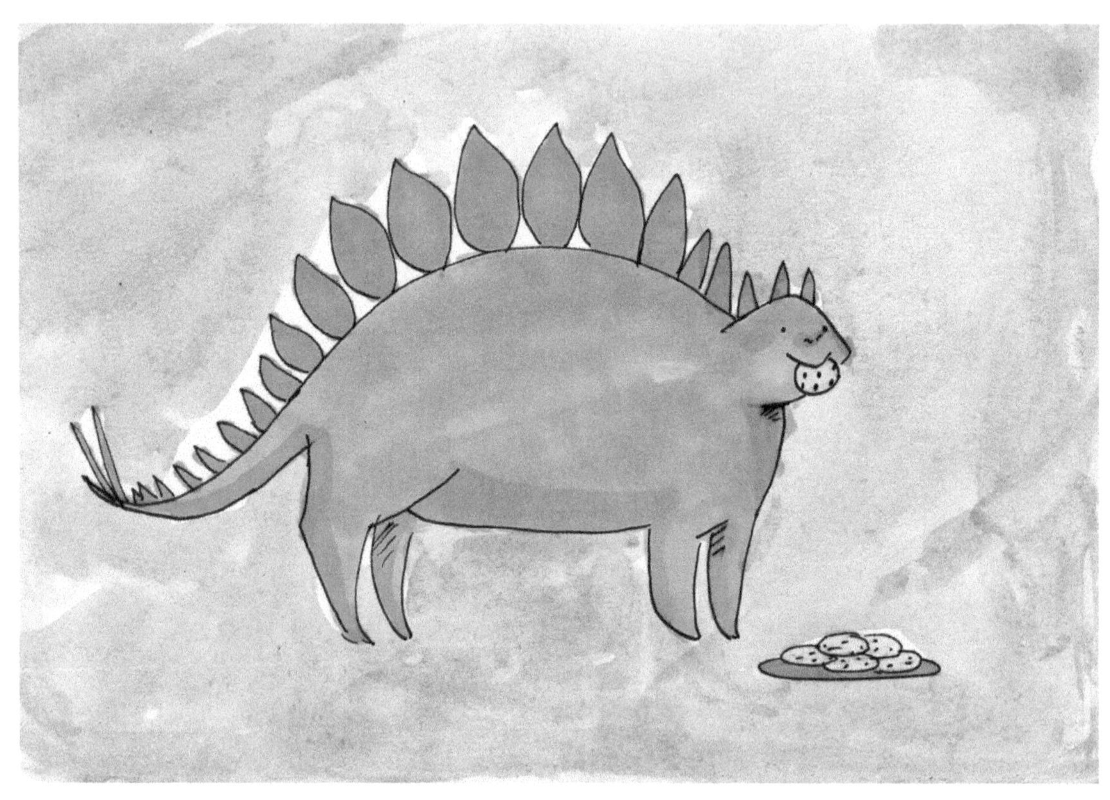

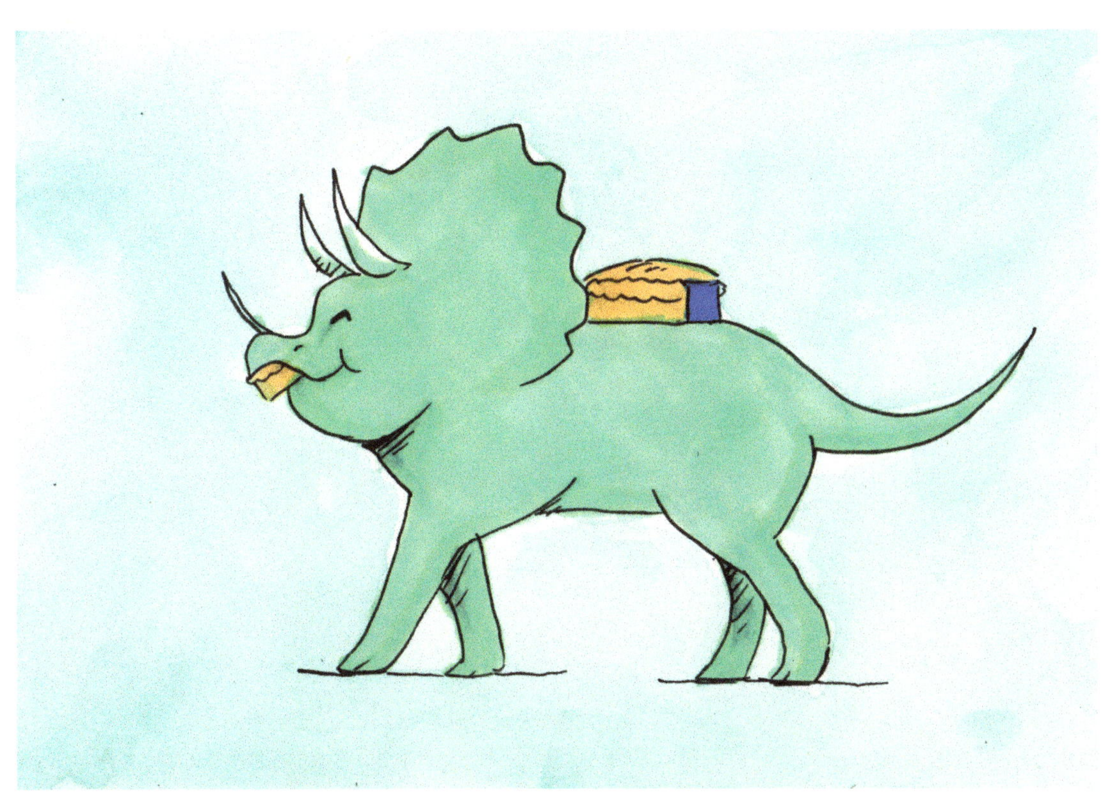

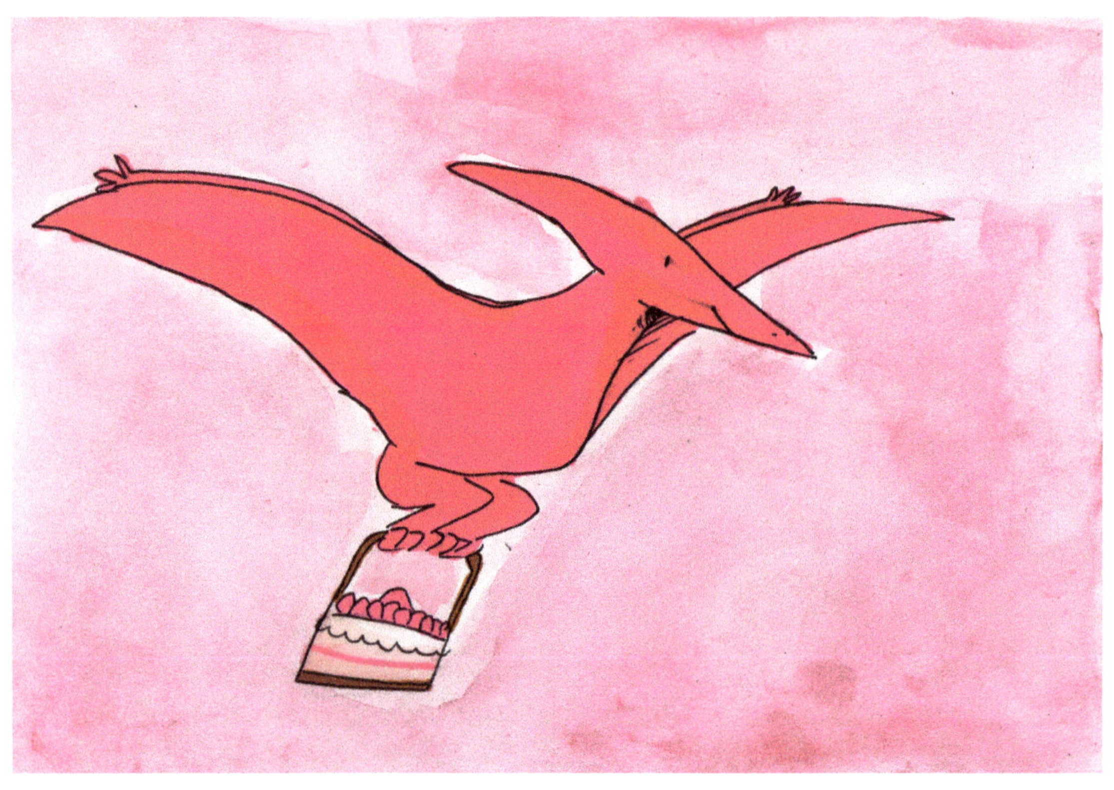

Mice and
Spice

Basil

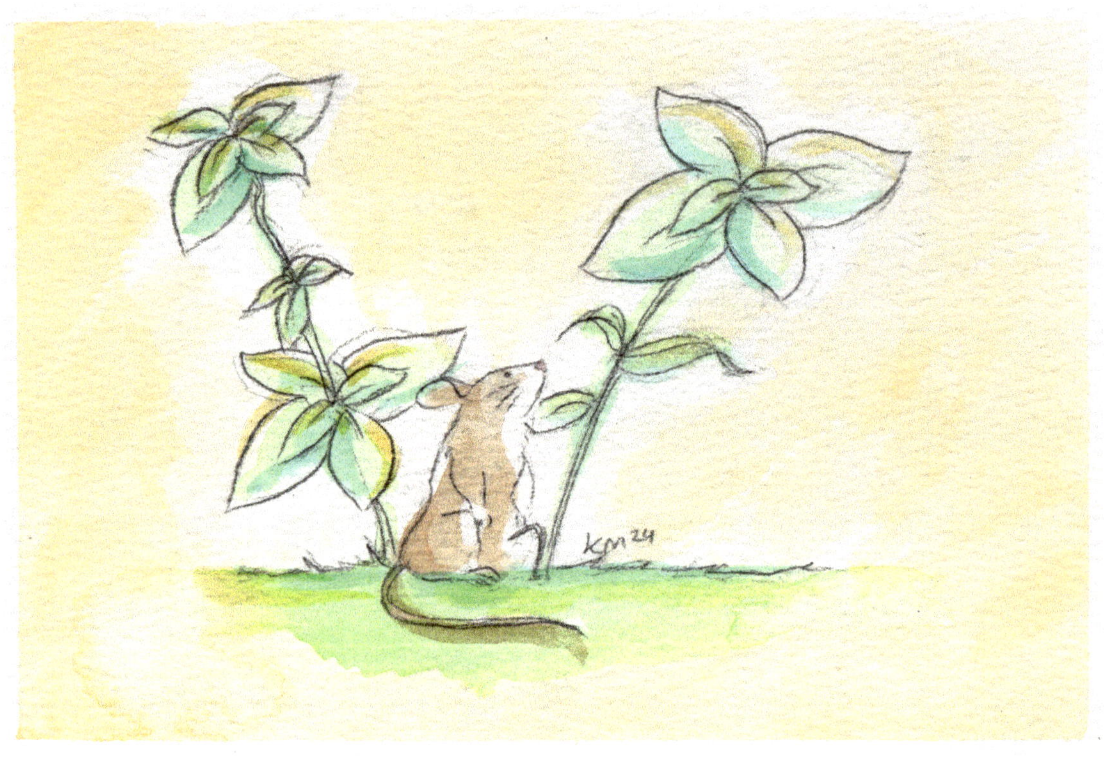

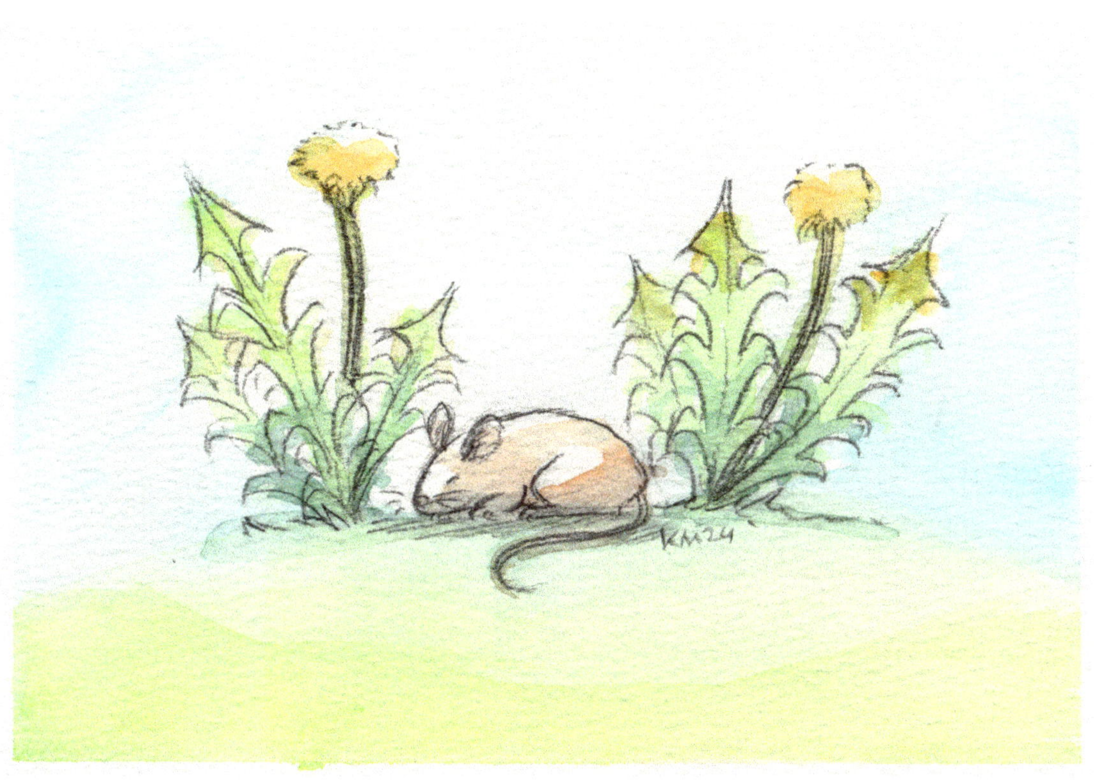

Dill

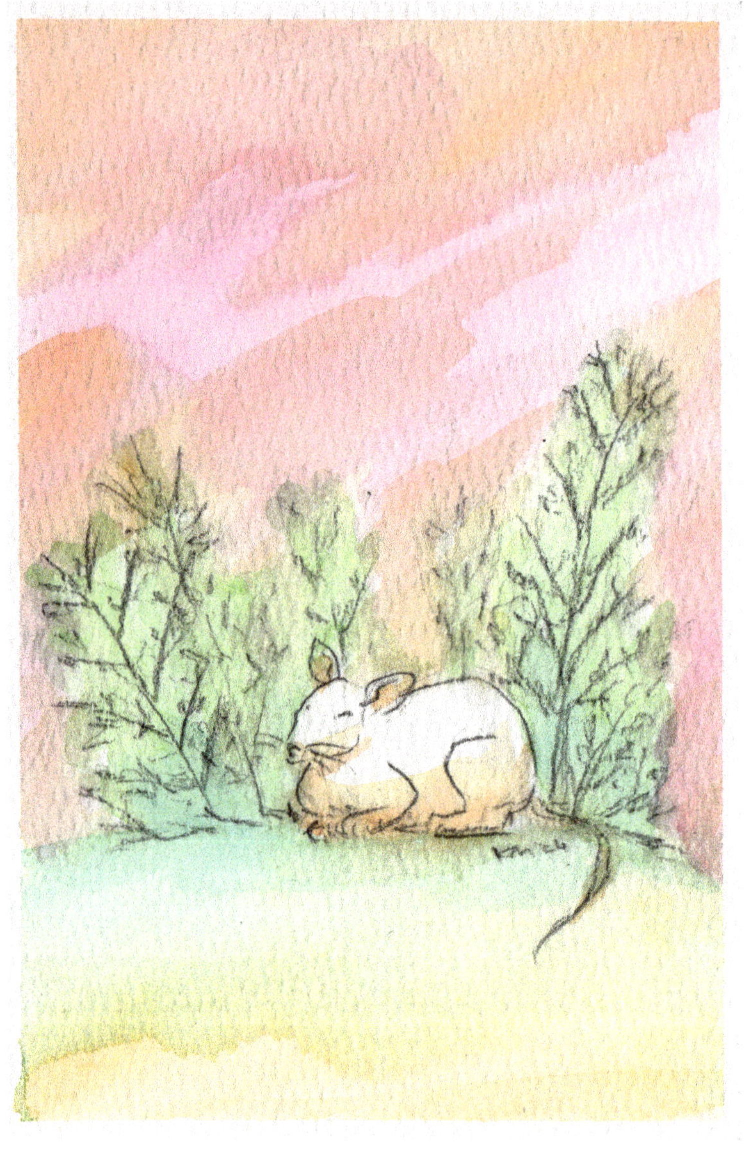

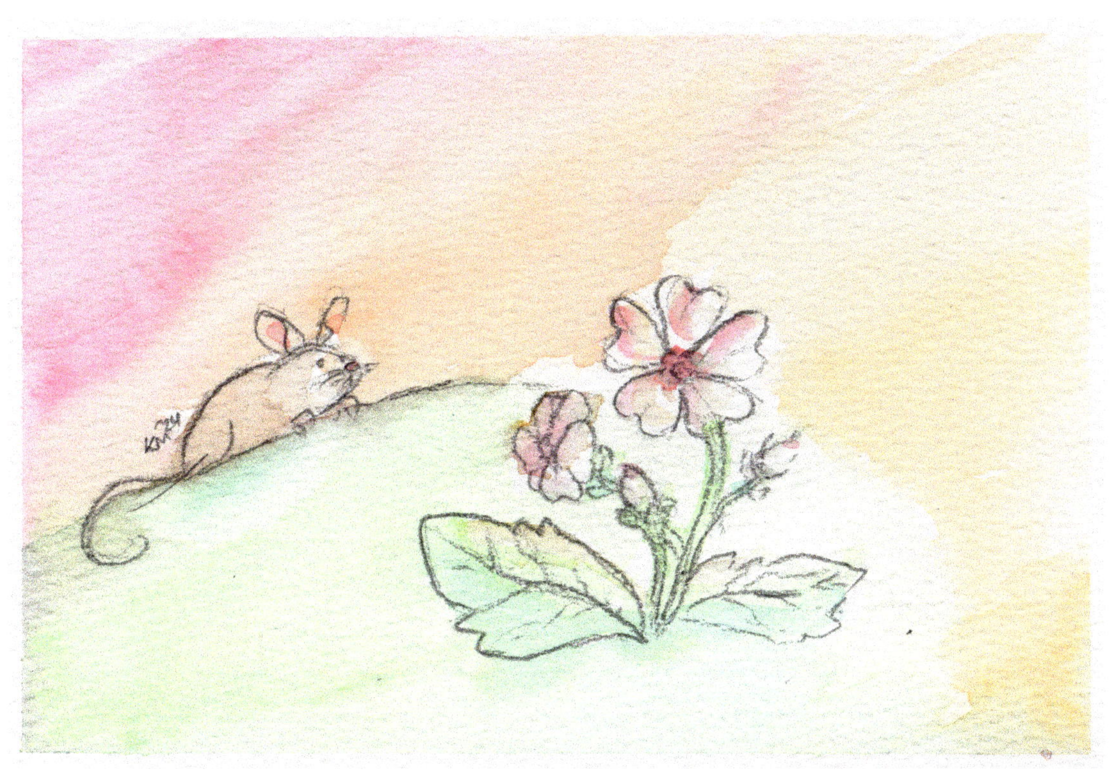

Red Clover

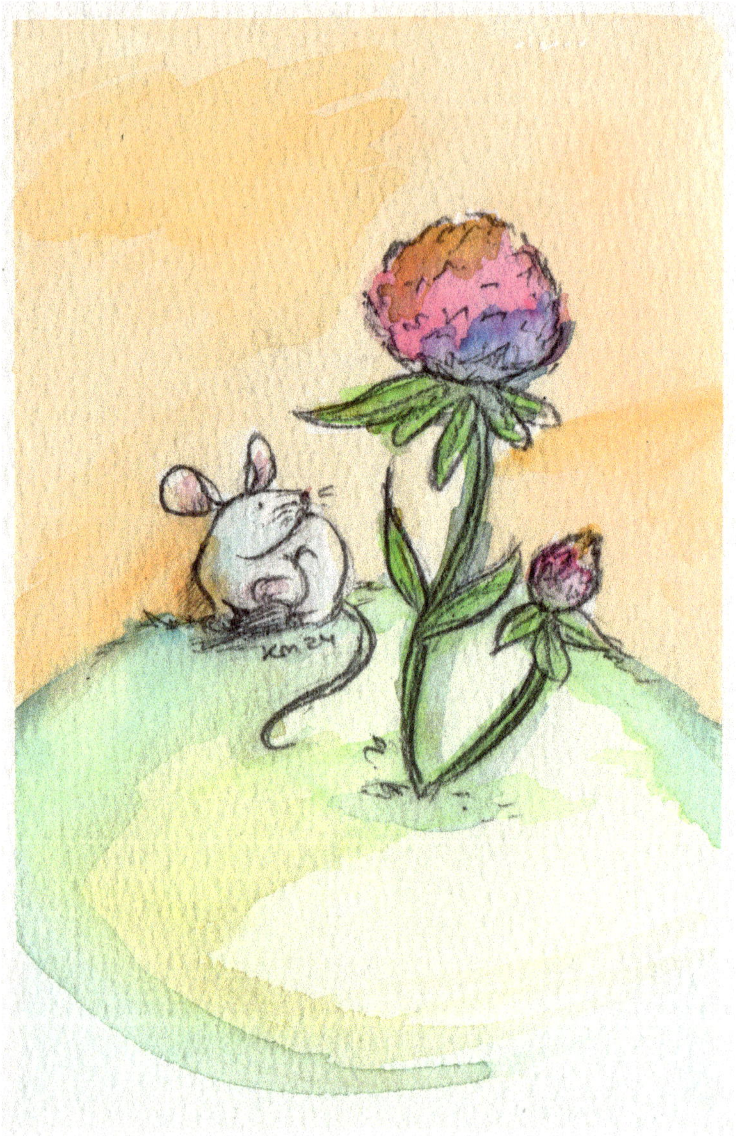

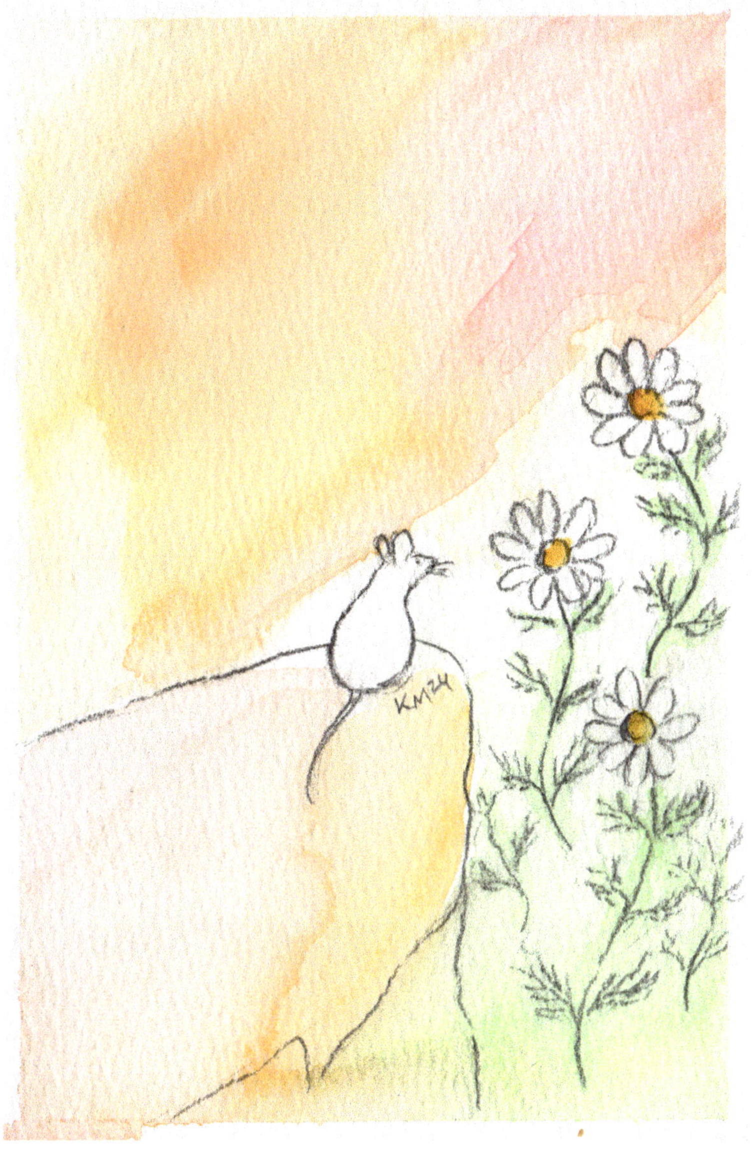

Chamomile

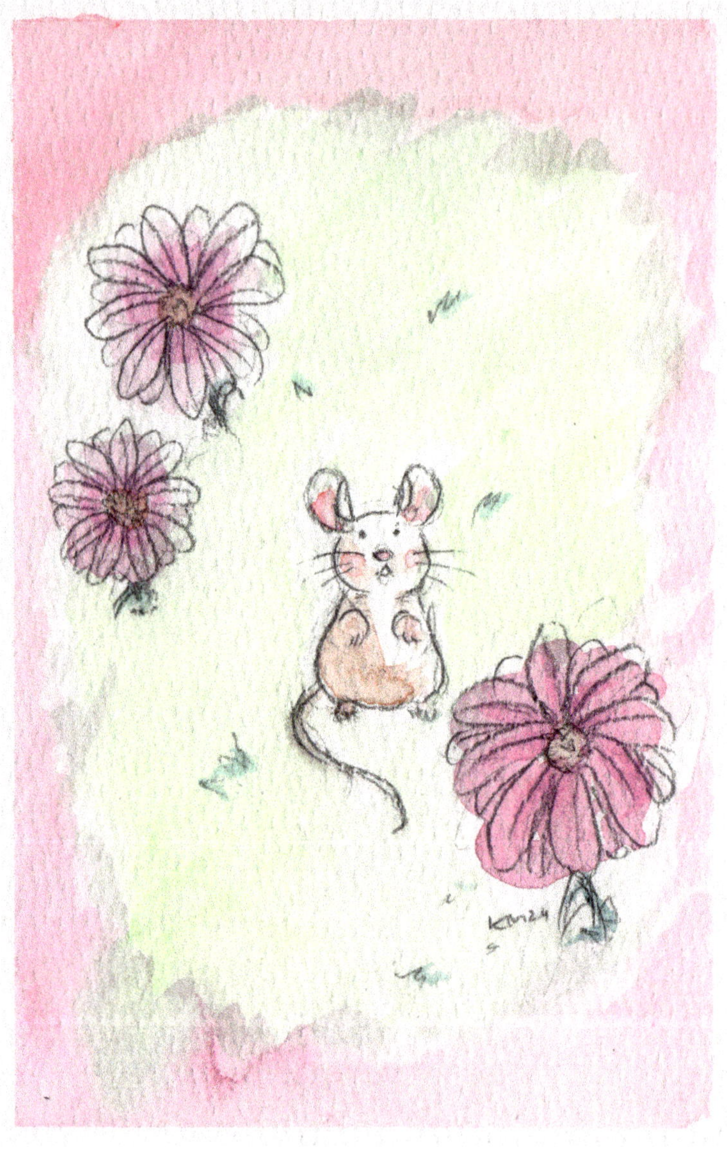

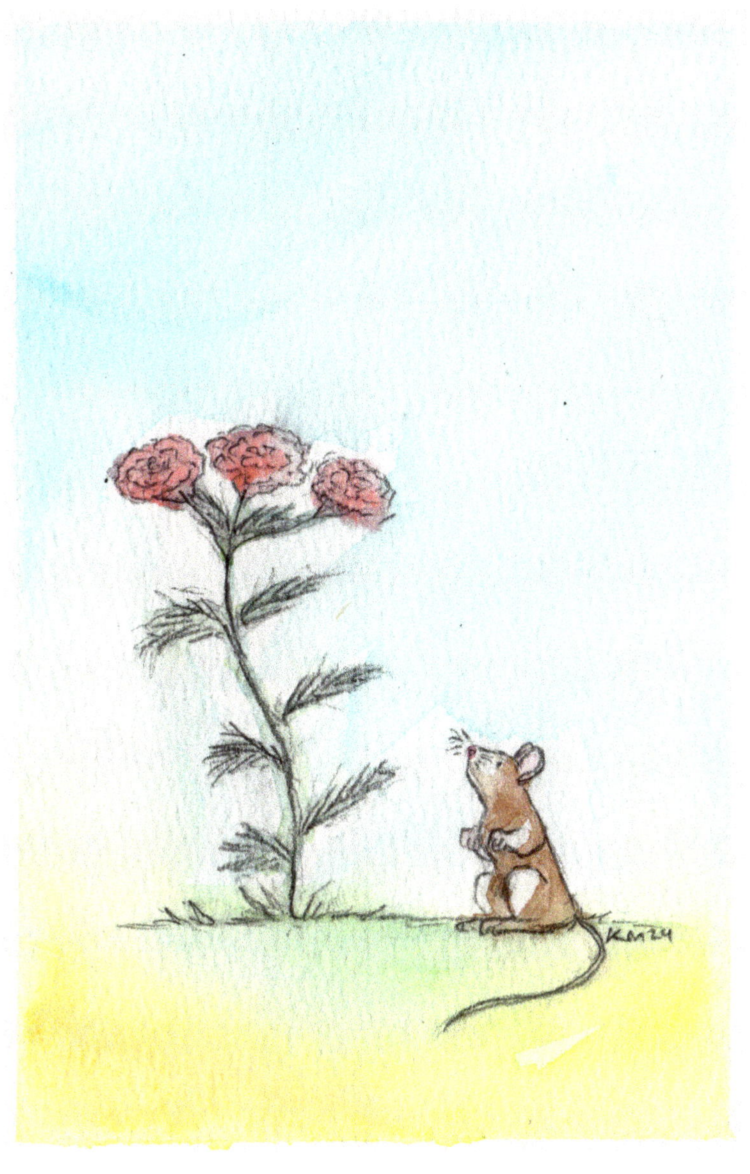

Planet

People

Earth

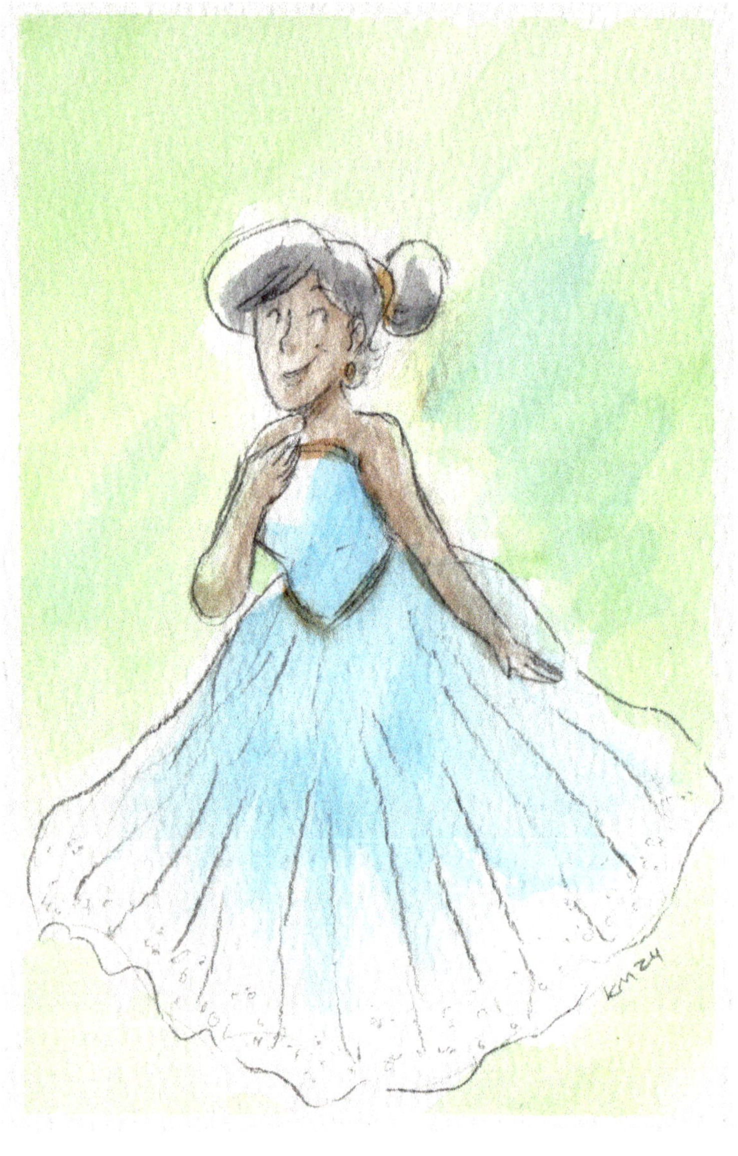

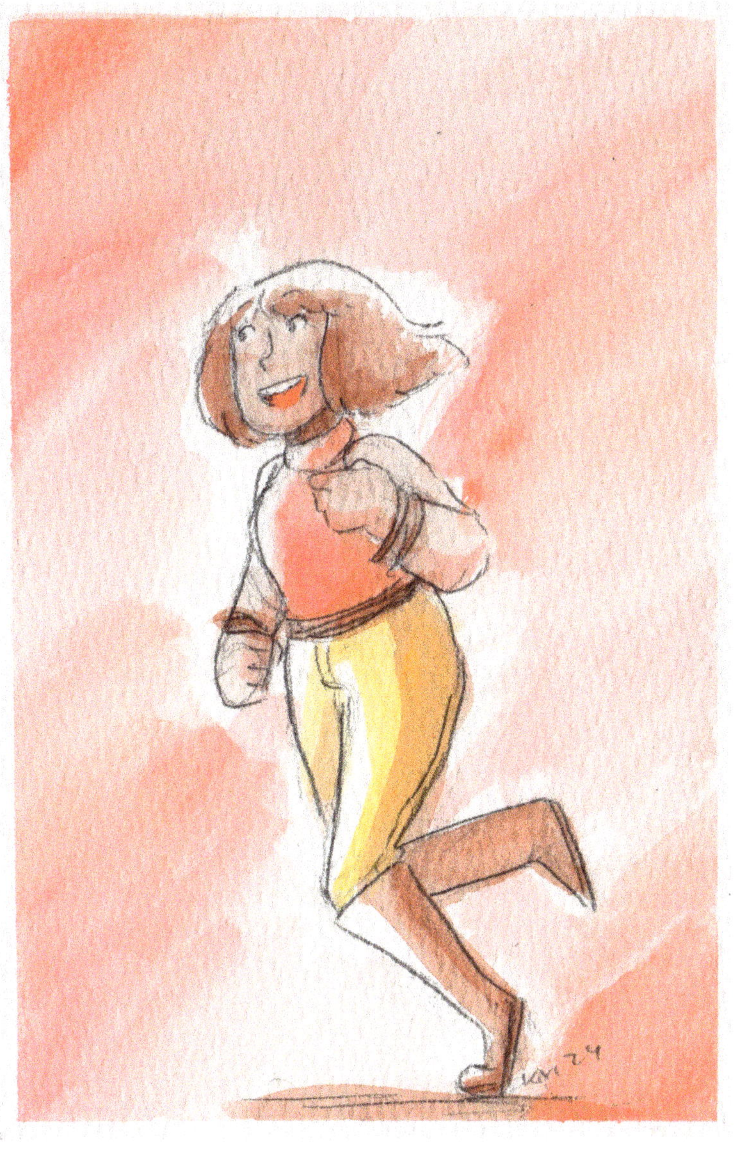

Mercury

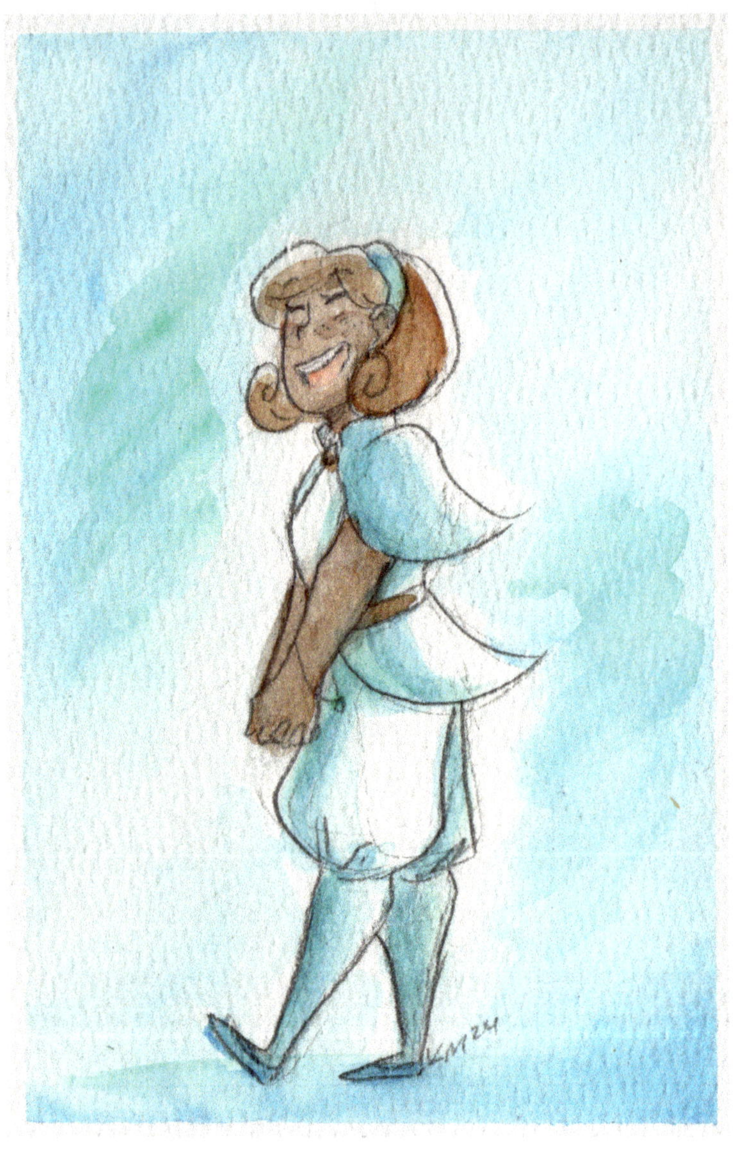

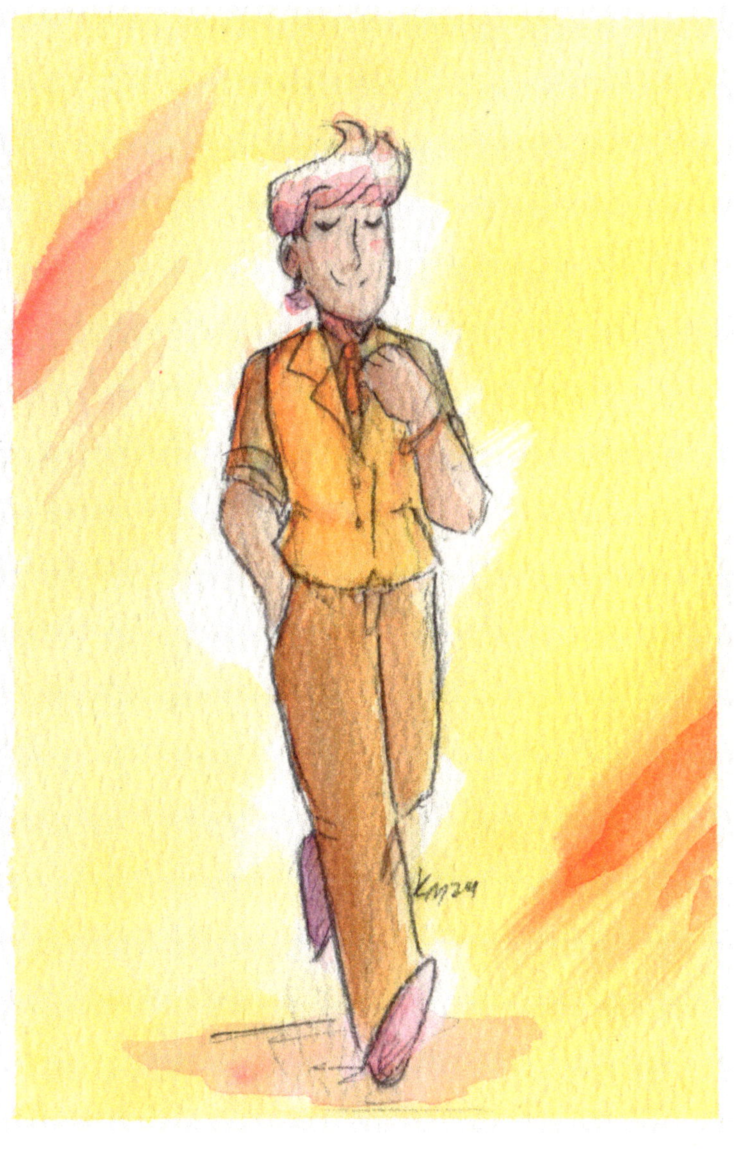

Uranus

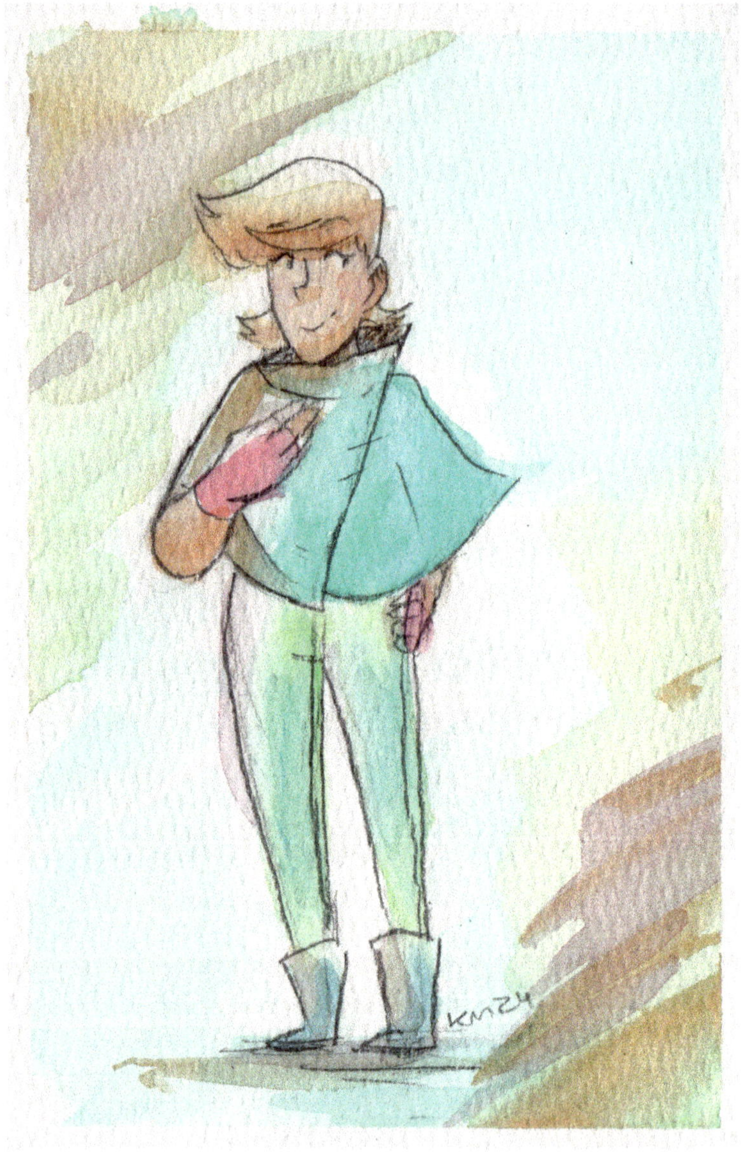

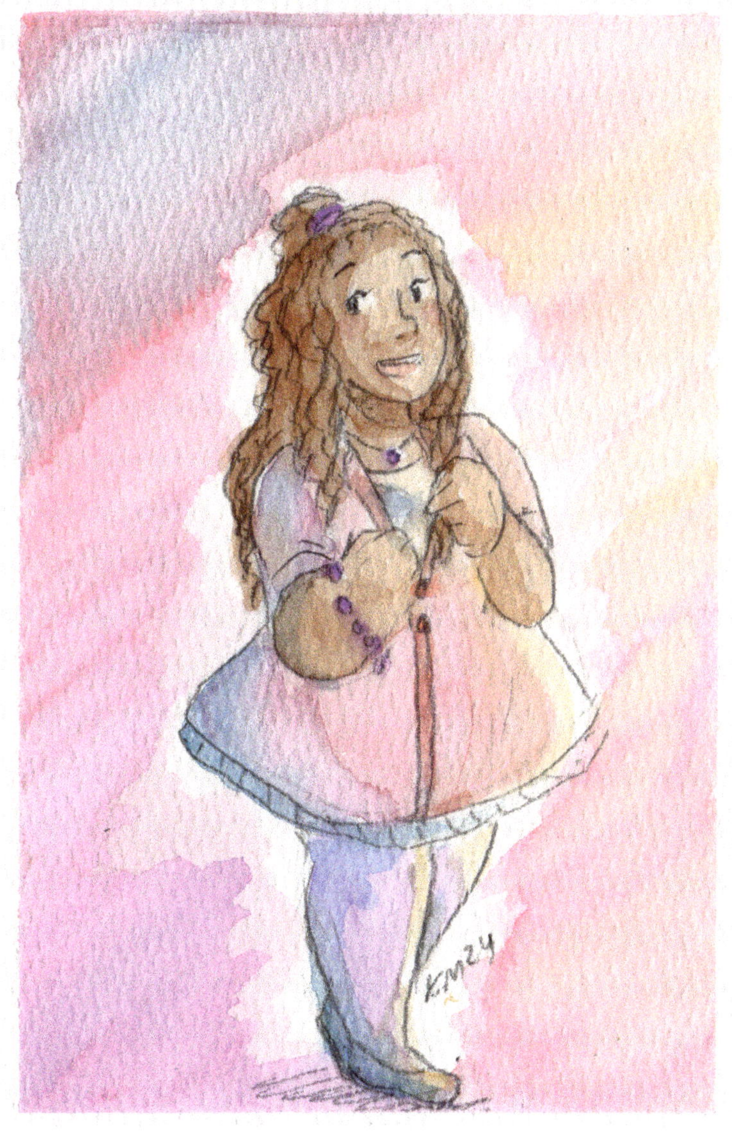

Neptune

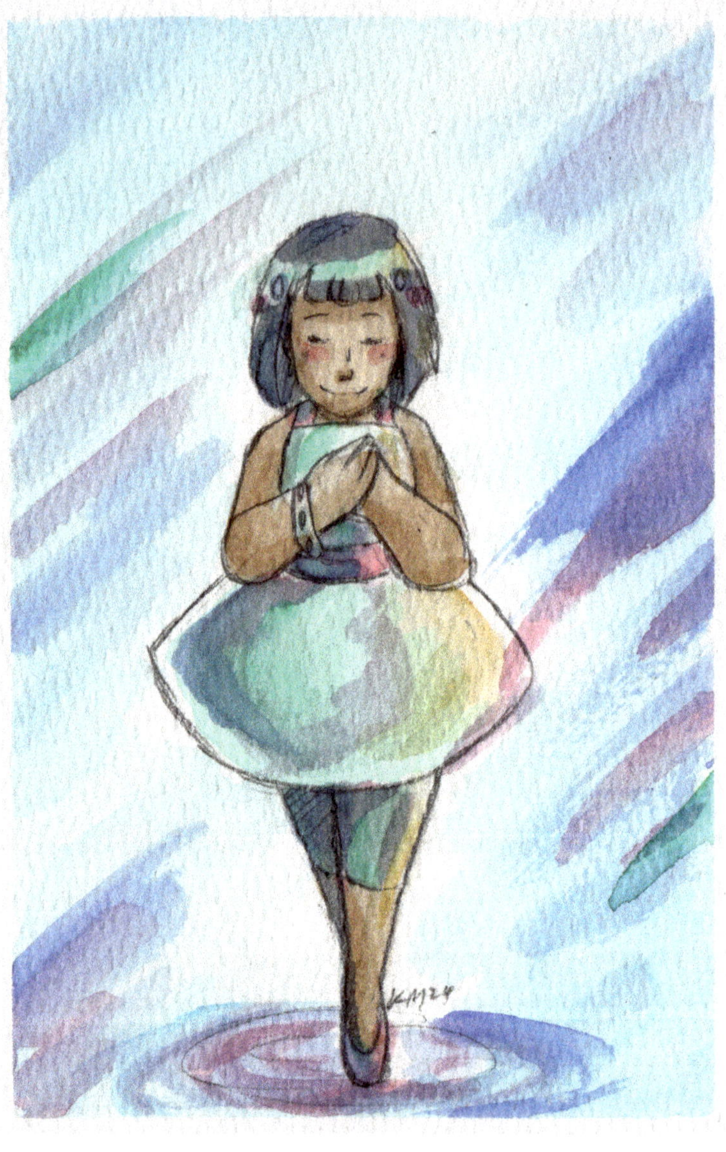

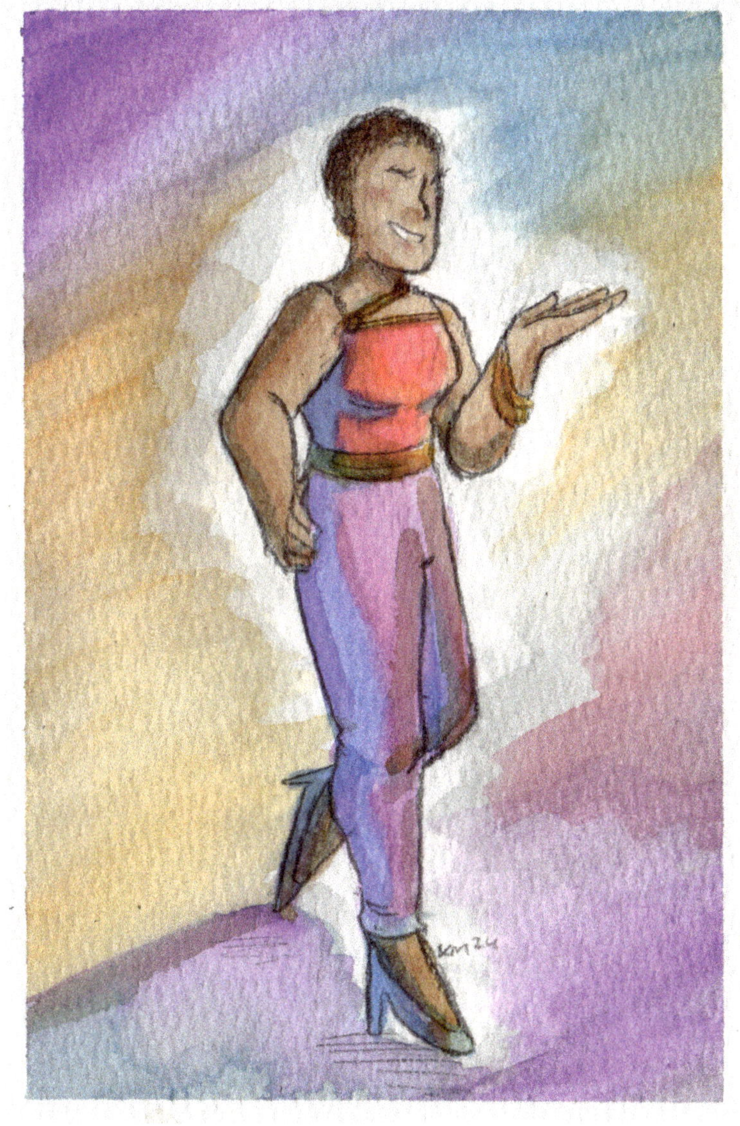

Pluto

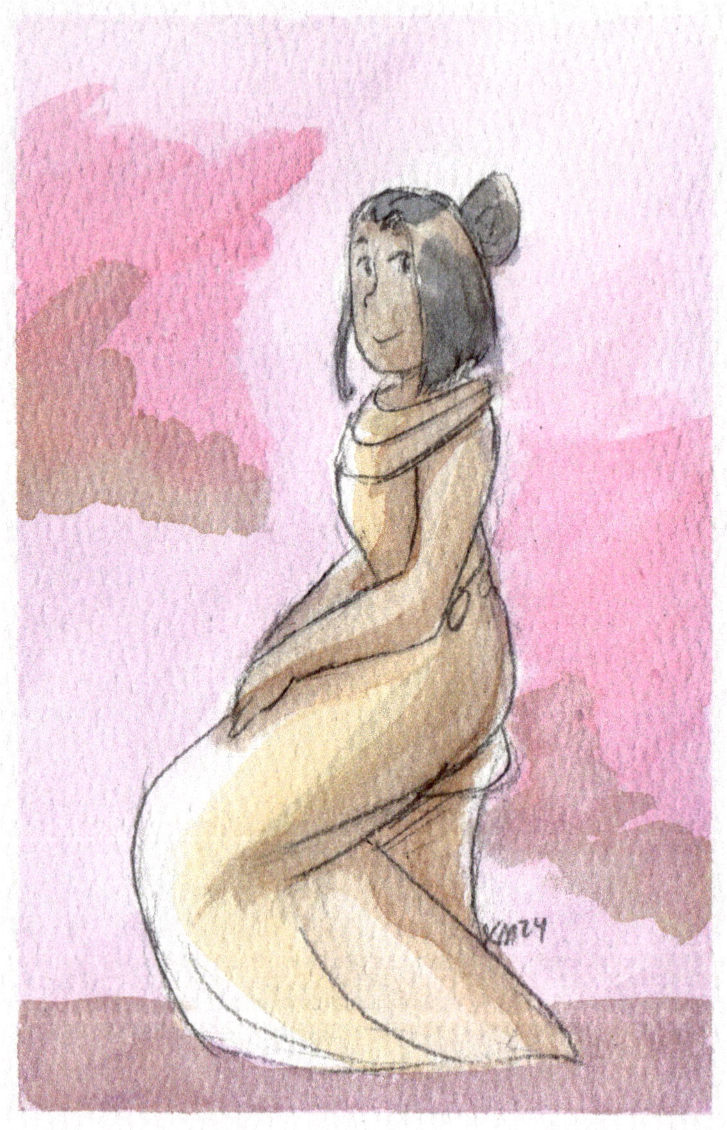

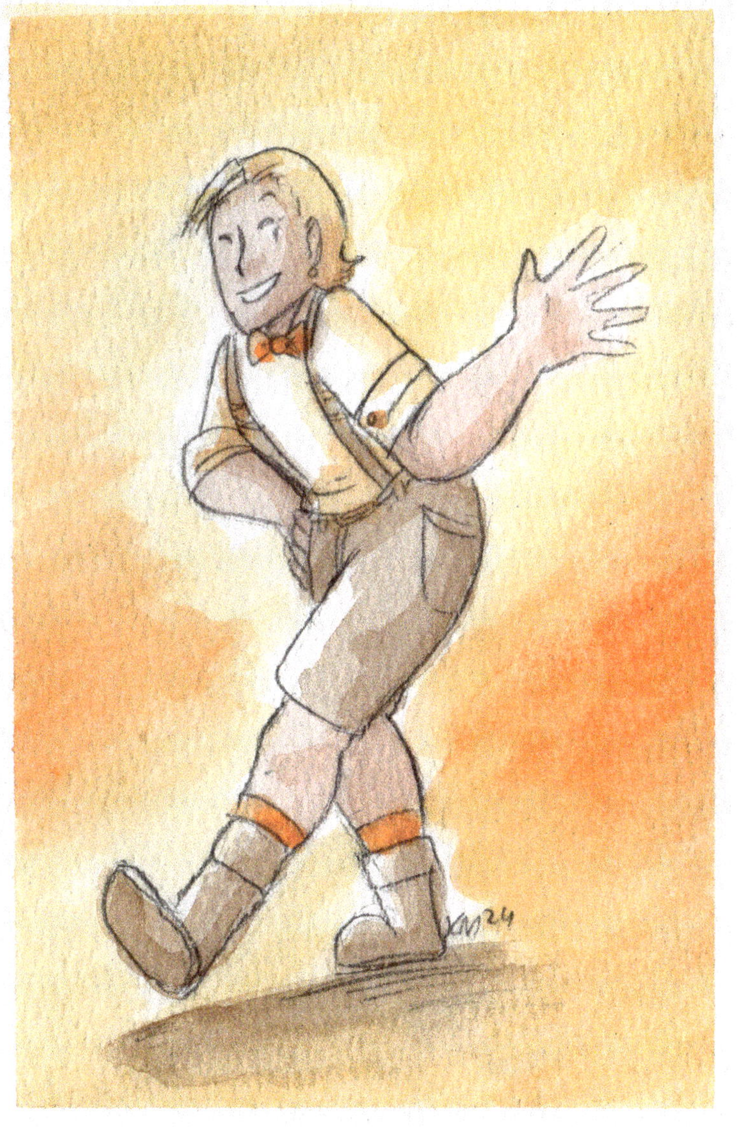

Snakes
in Hats

Python
Top Hat

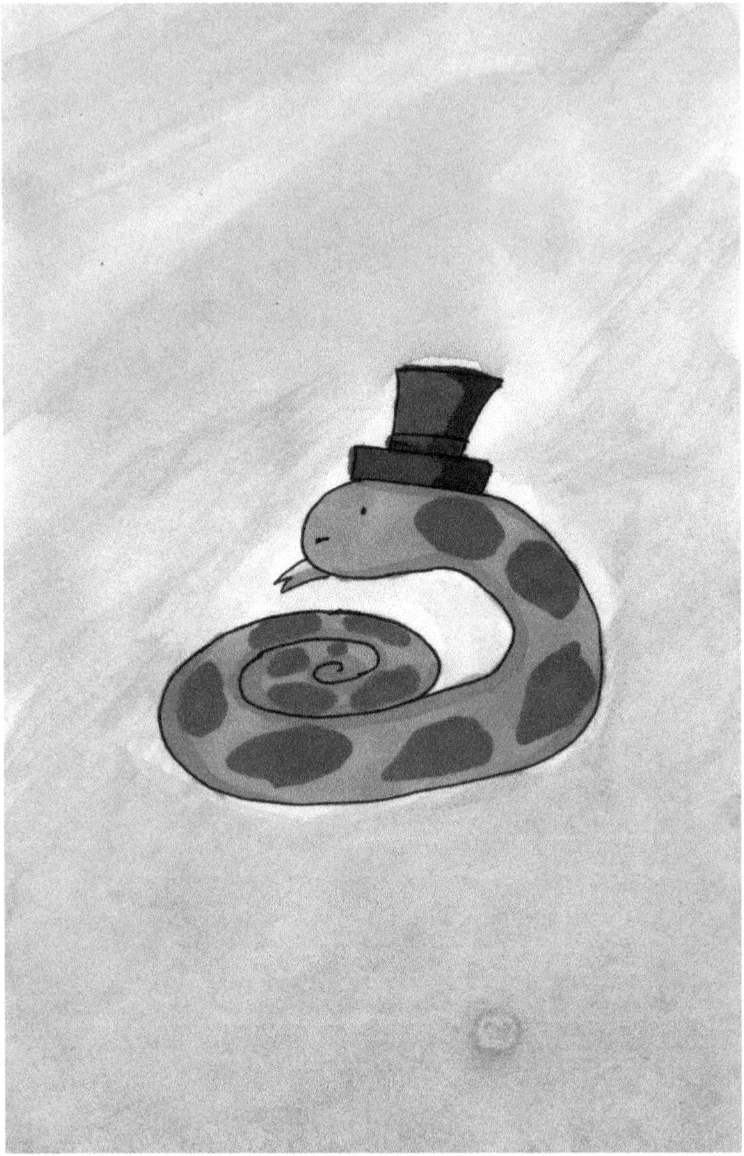

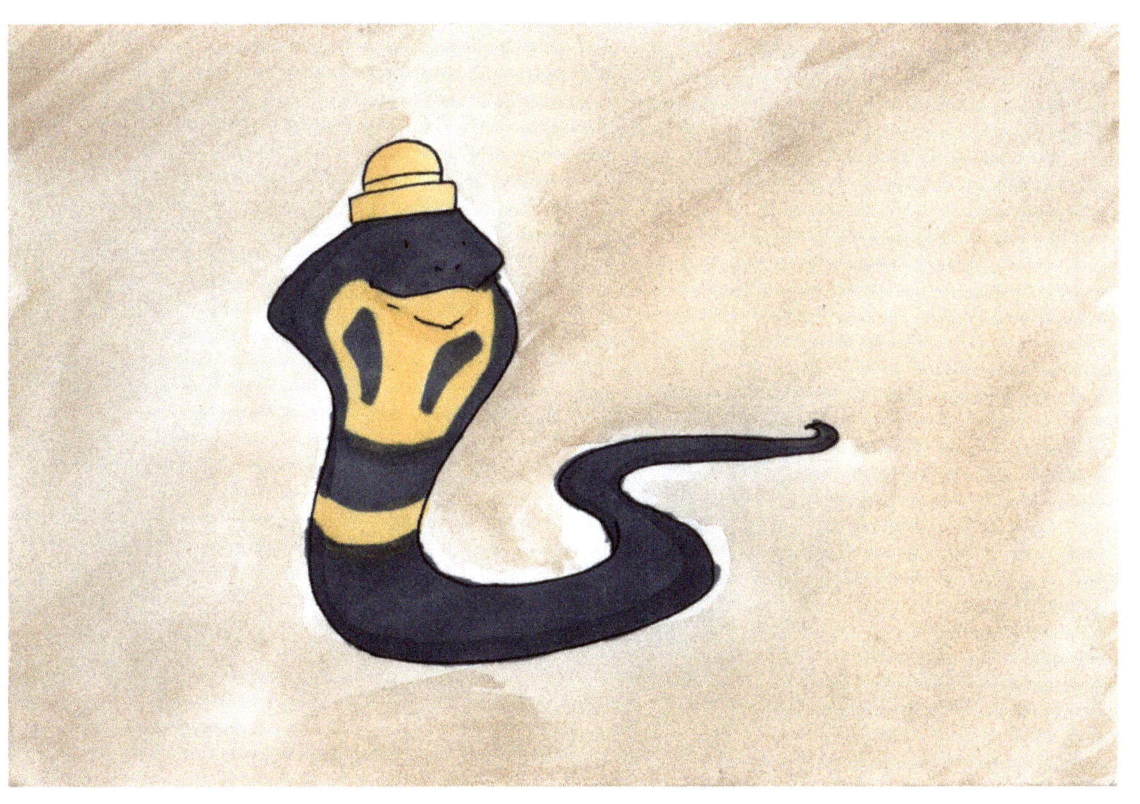

Garter Snake Earmuffs

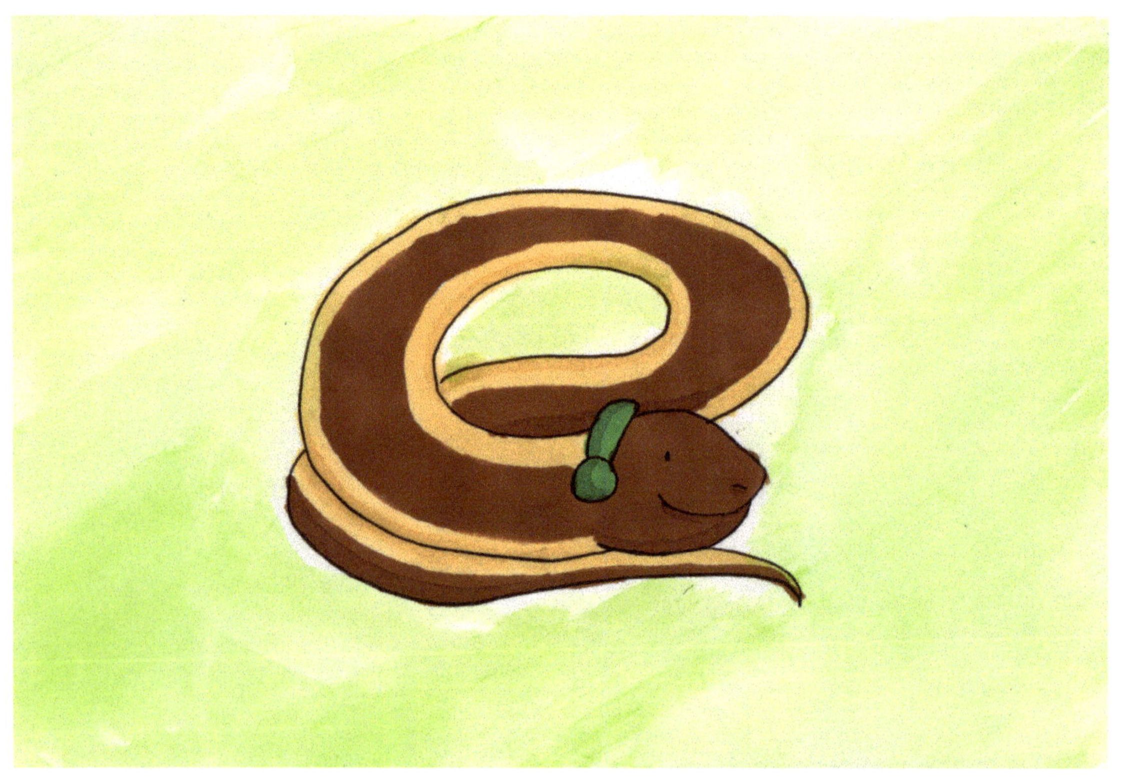

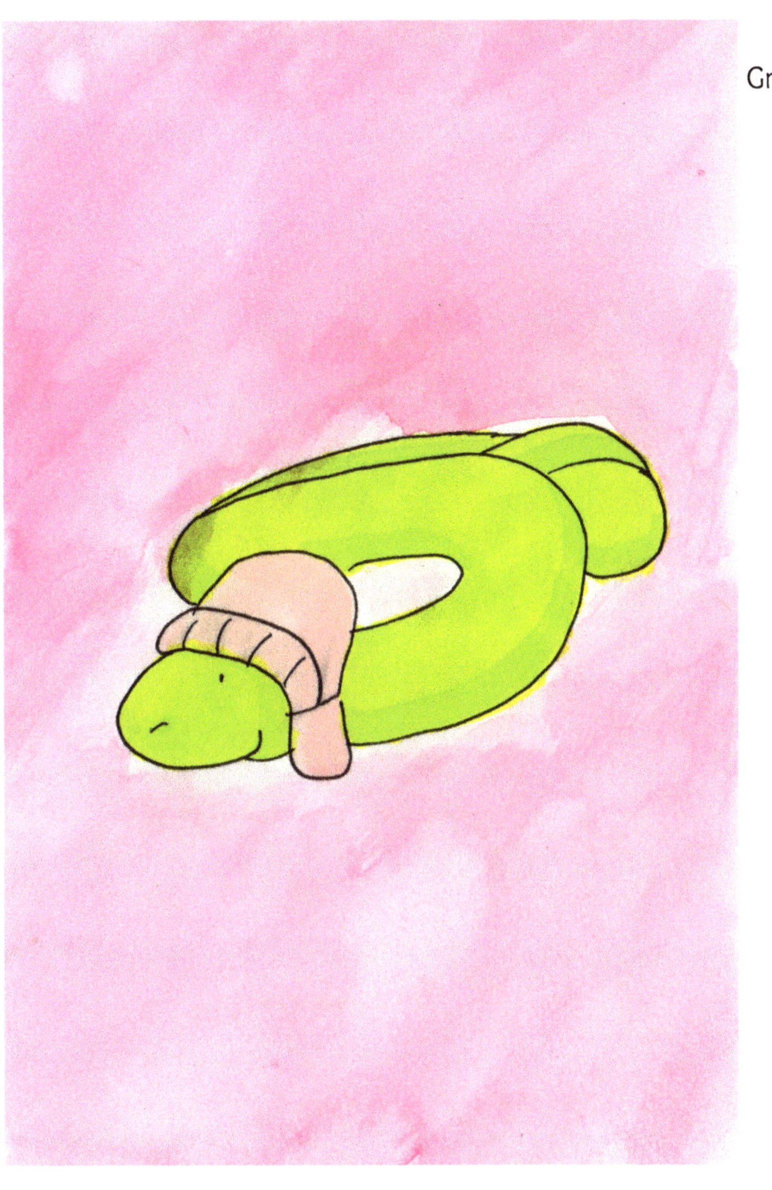

Eastern
Green Mamba
Beanie

Anaconda
Sun Hat

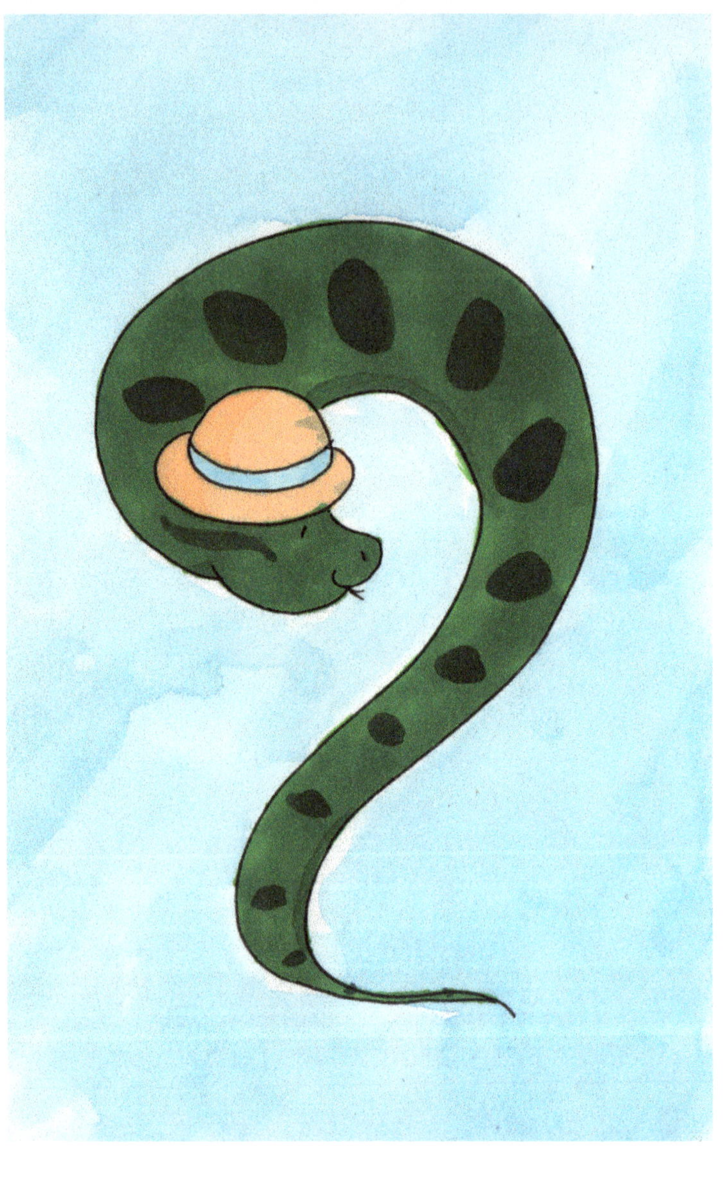

Elemental
Dragons

Sky

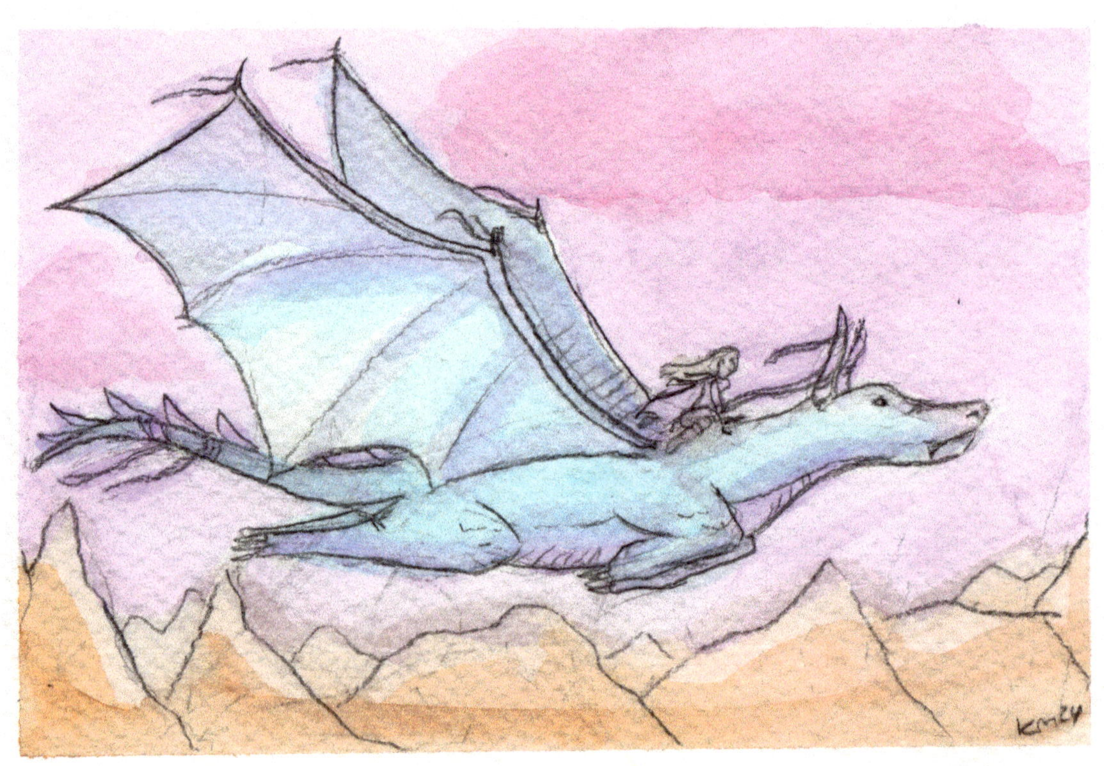

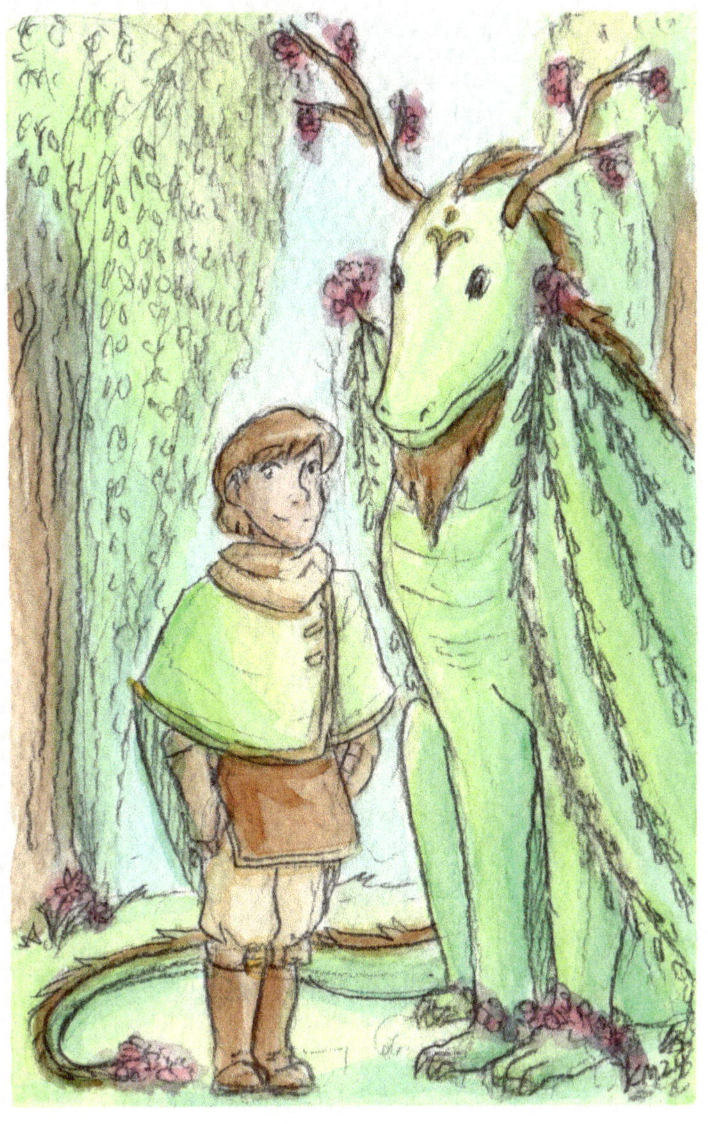

Fire

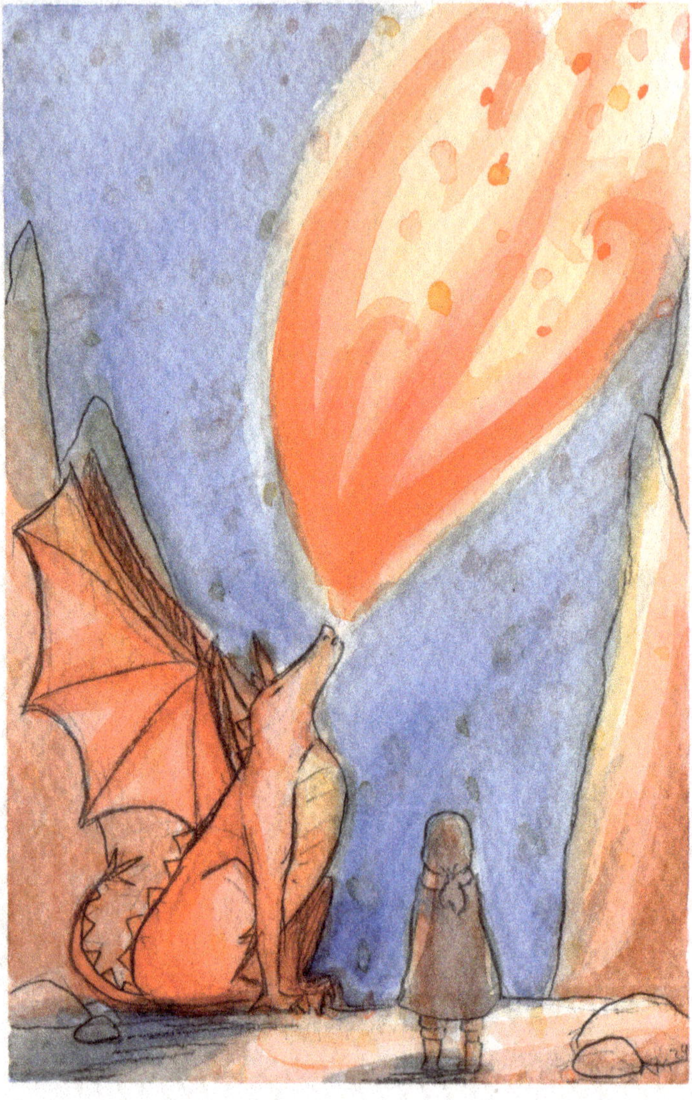

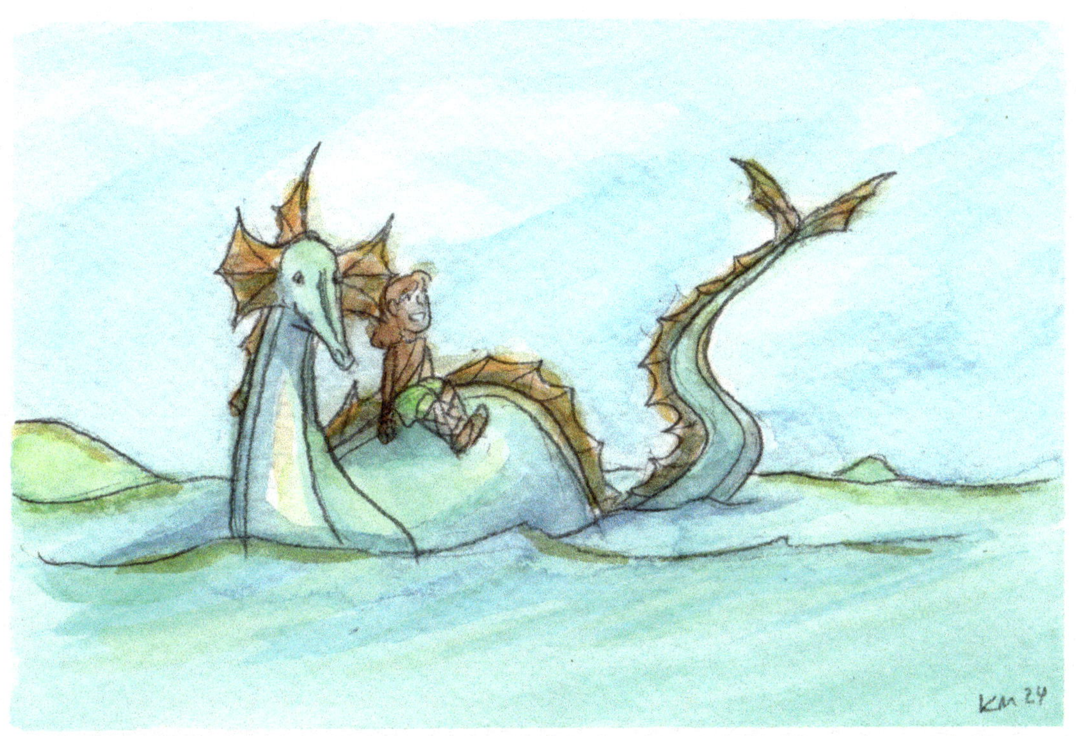

Stone

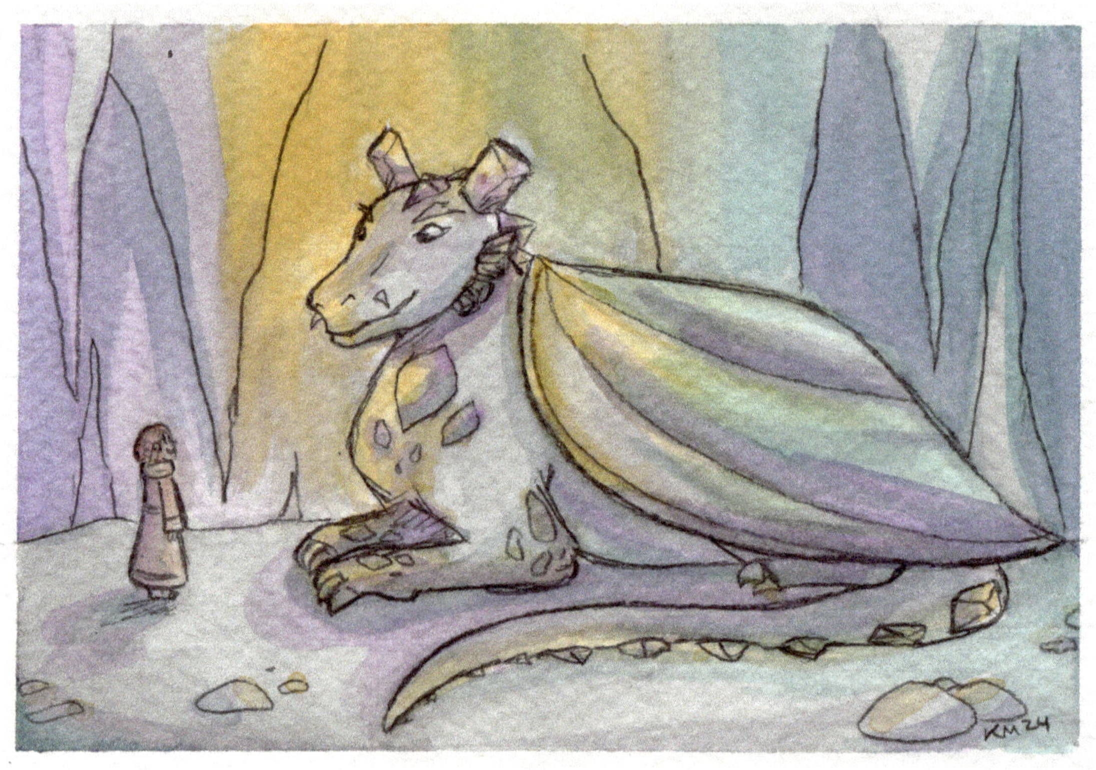

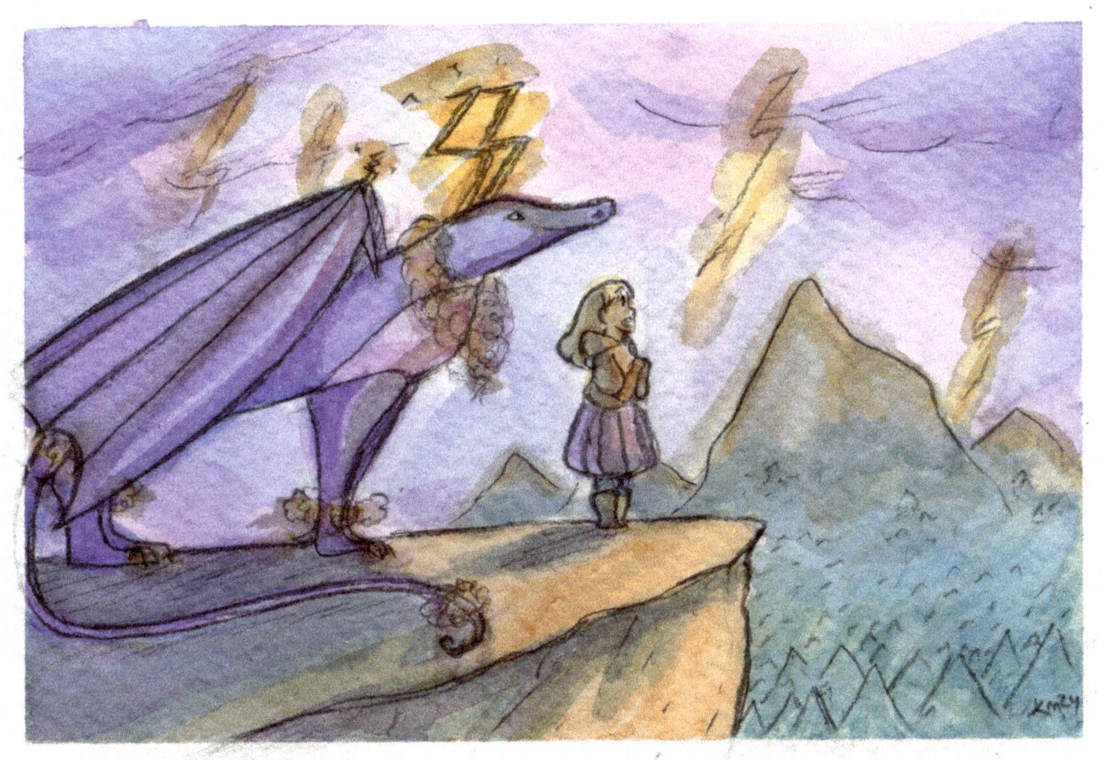

Cloud Wizards

Cirrus

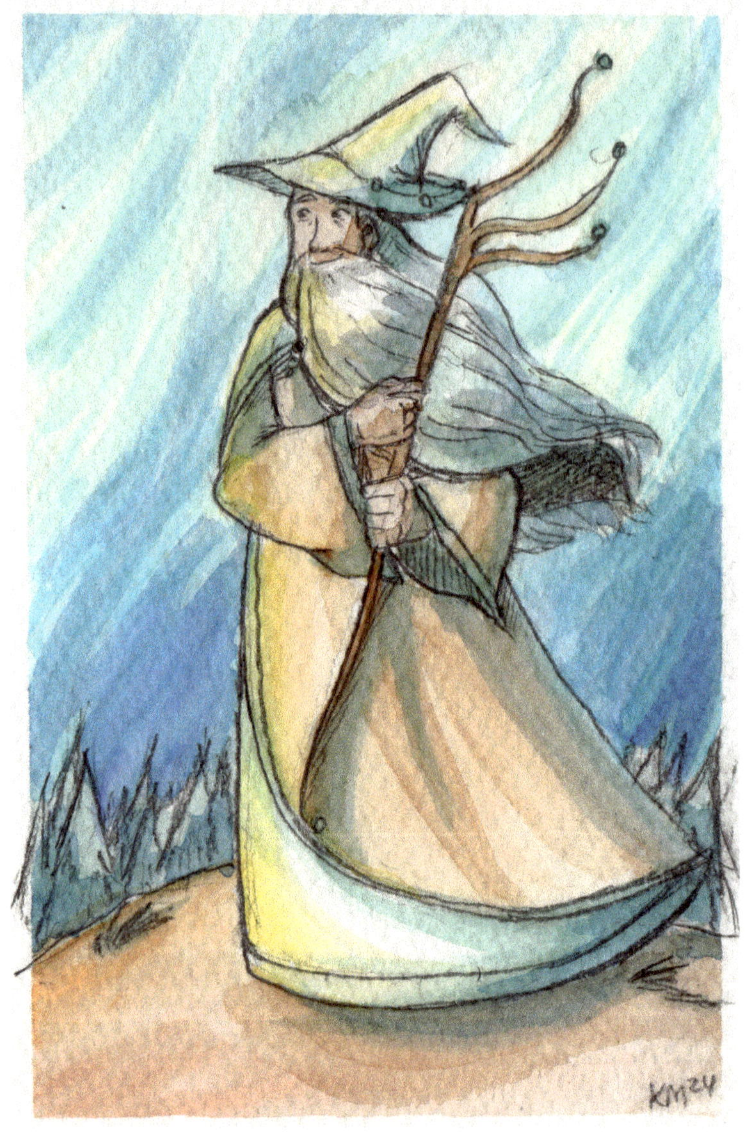

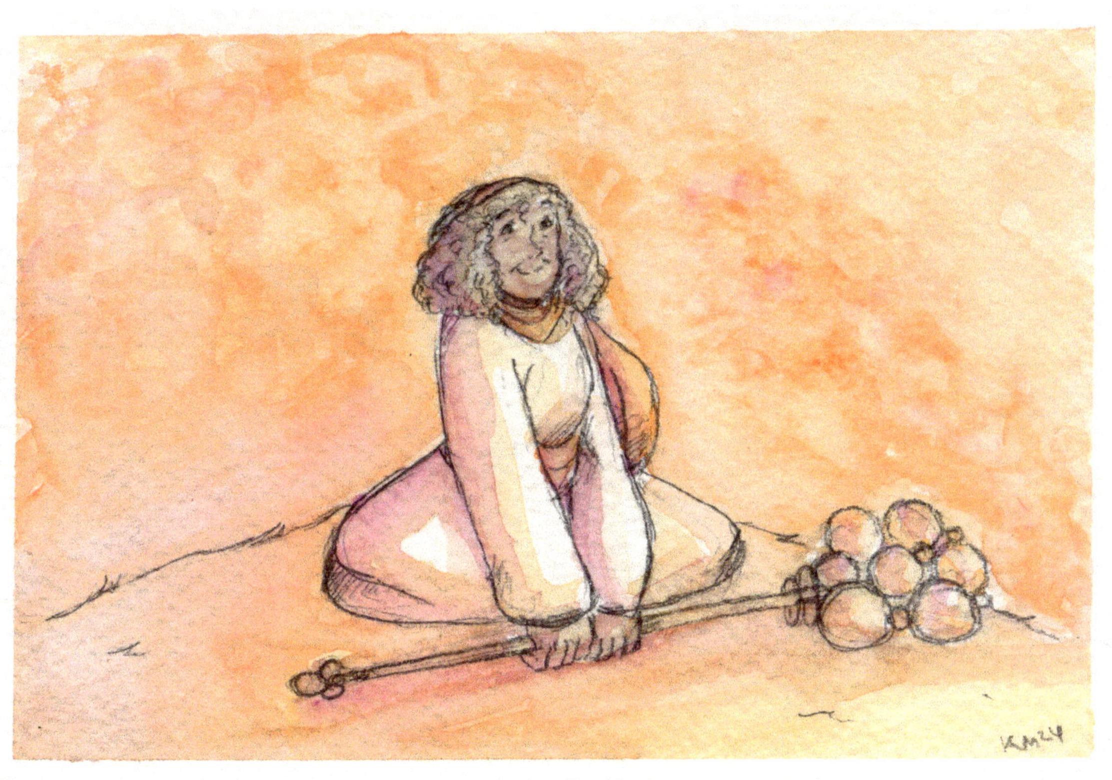

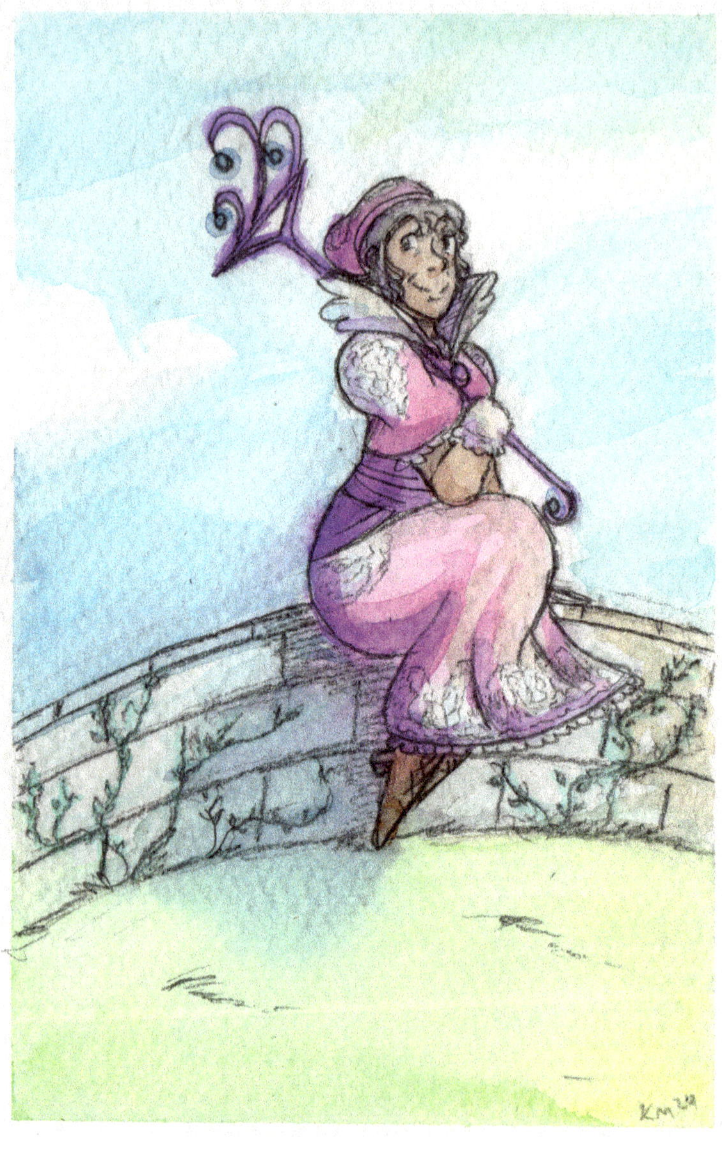

Cumulus

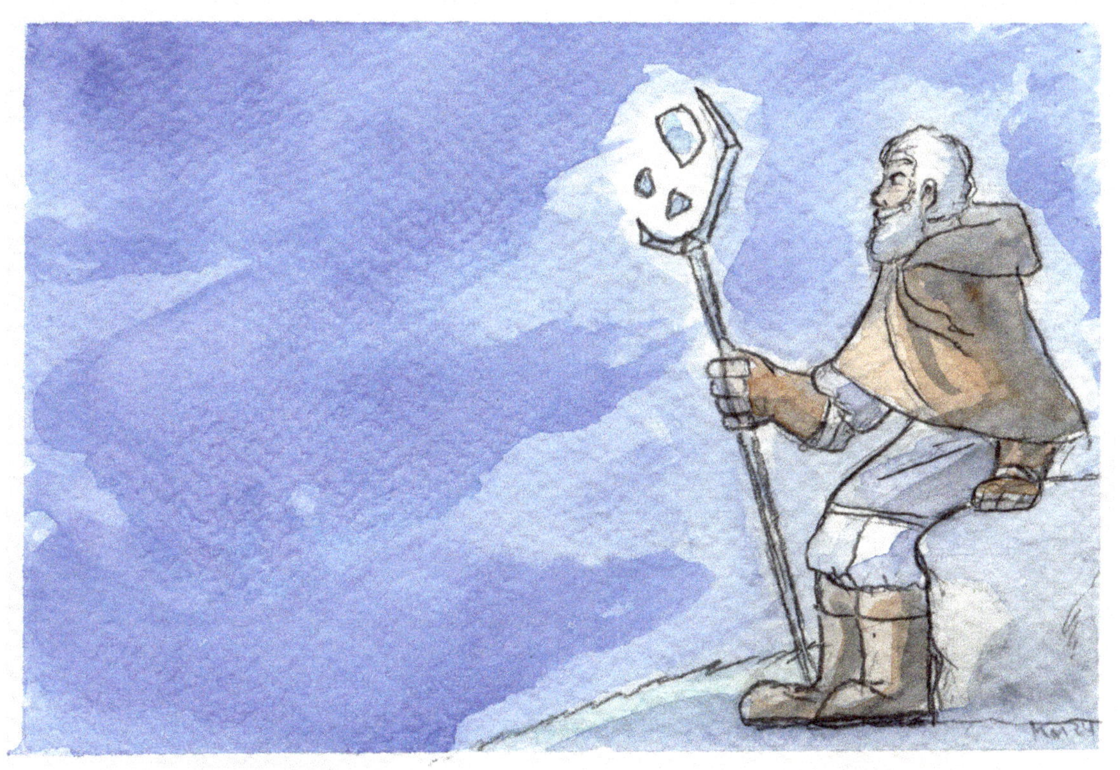

Cumulo-
nimbus

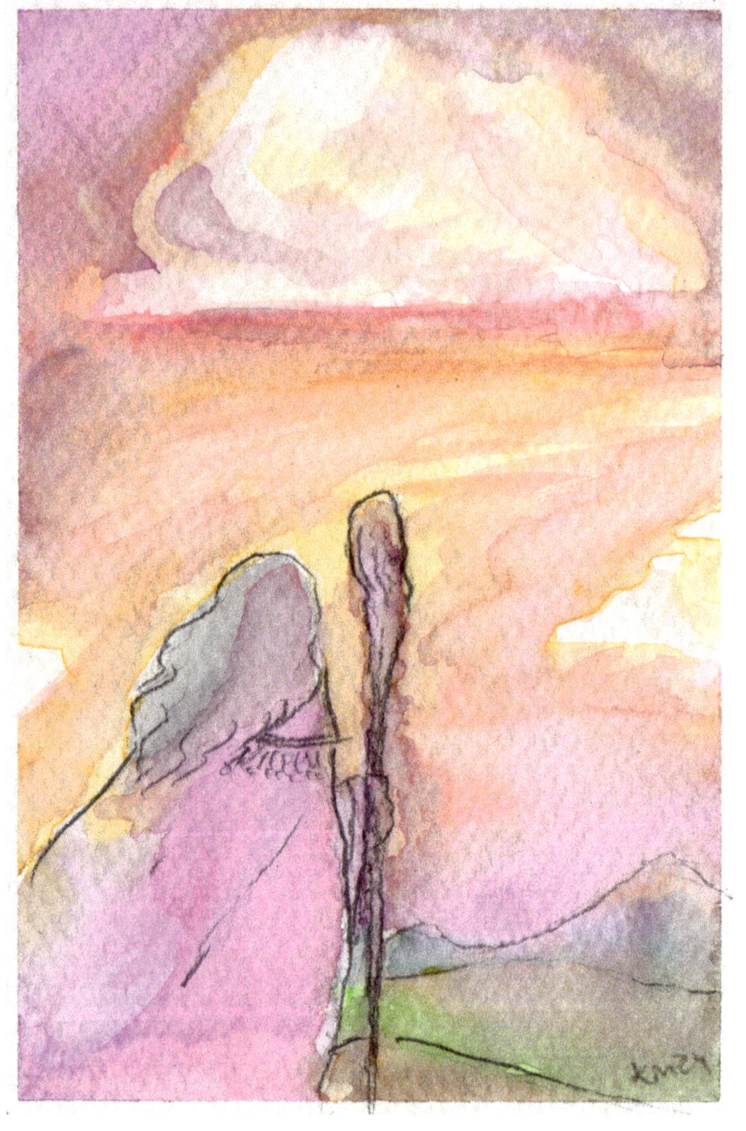

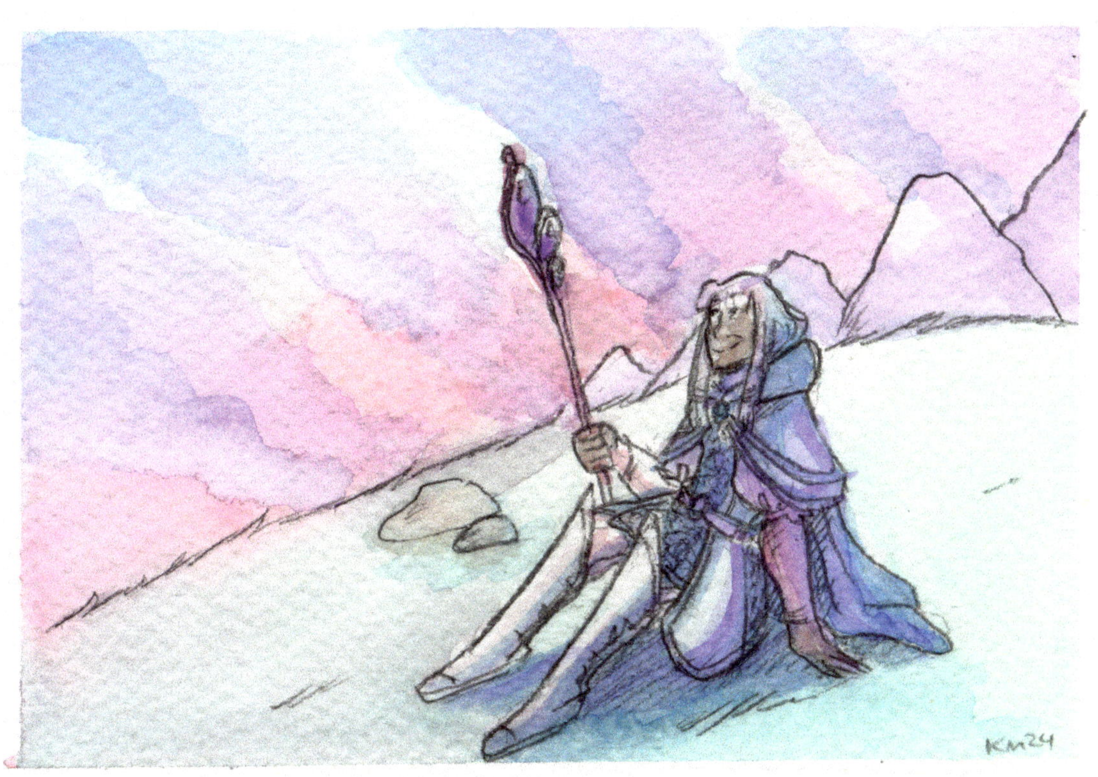

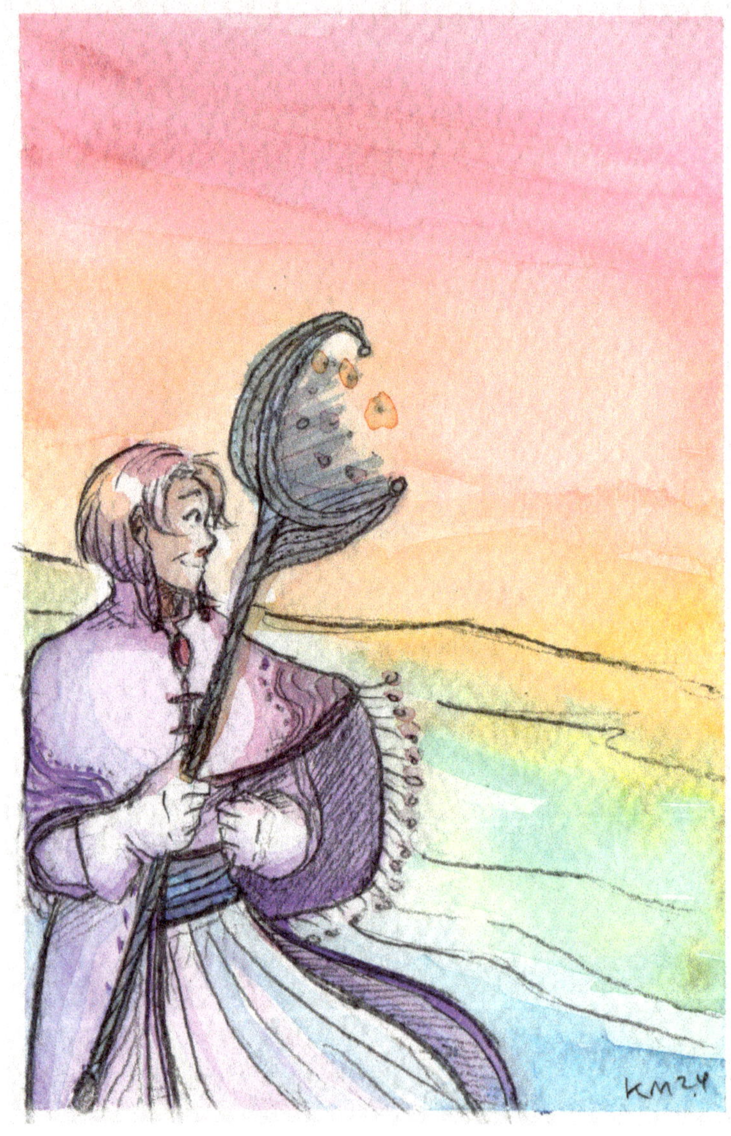

Stratus

Cactus

Cats

Rabbit Ear
Cactus

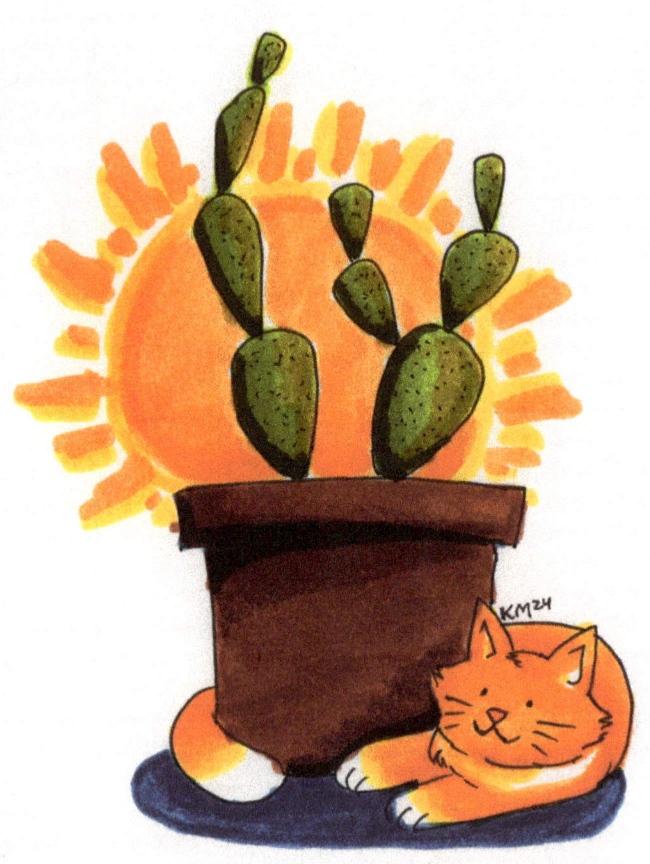

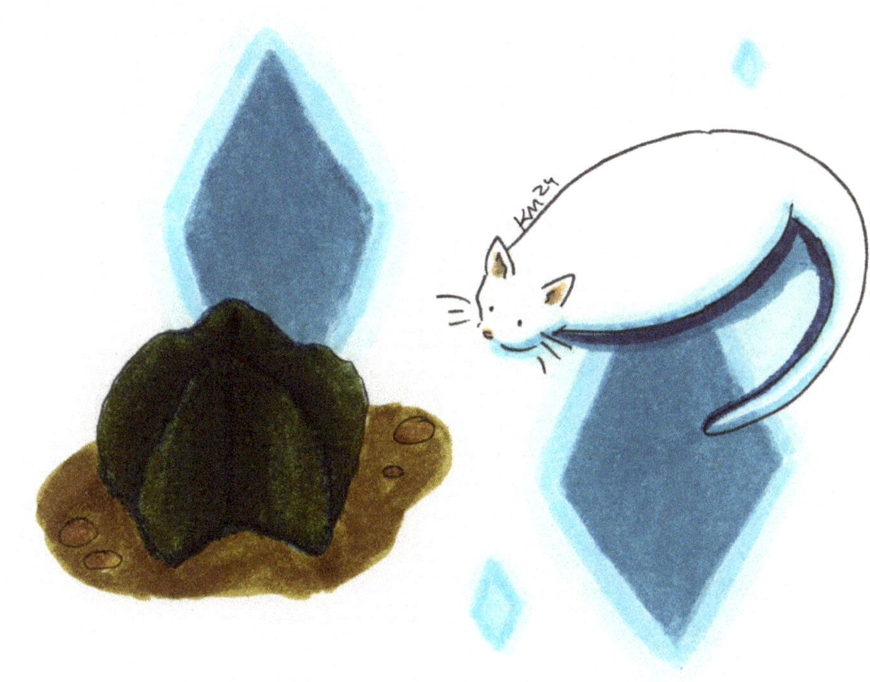

Panda Plant

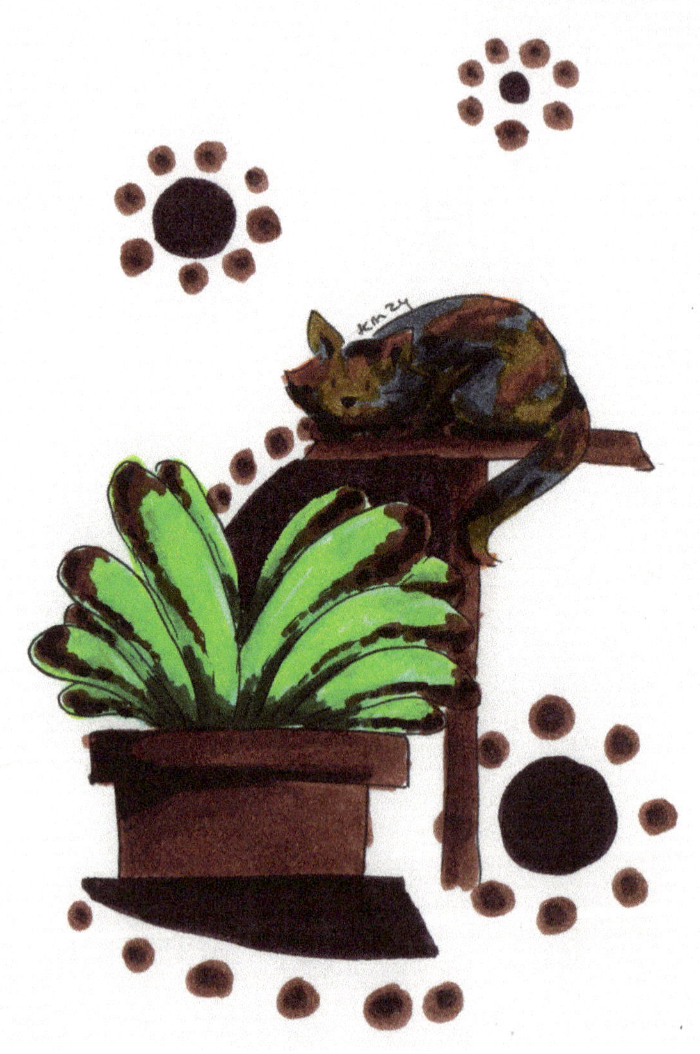

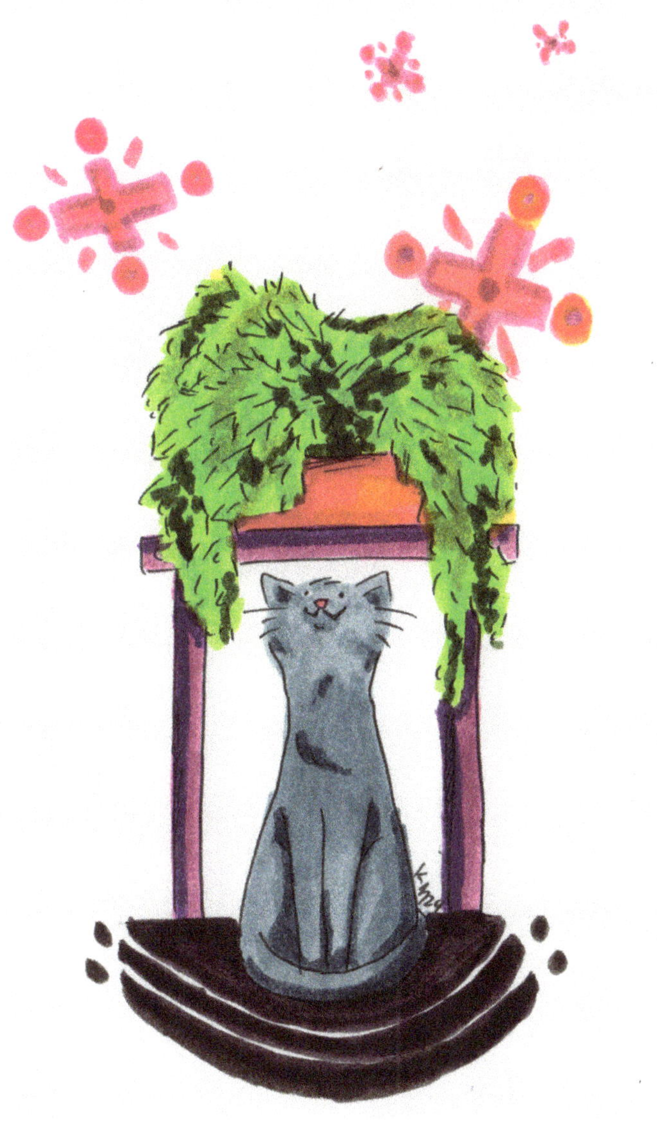

Fairy Tale
Castle Cactus

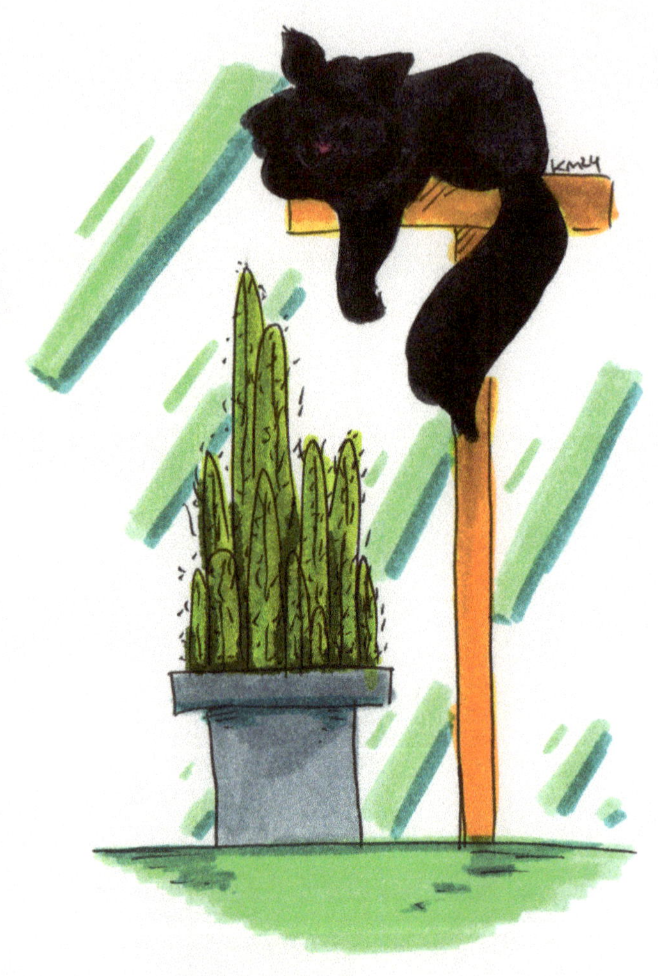

Rainbow
Umbrellas

Pink

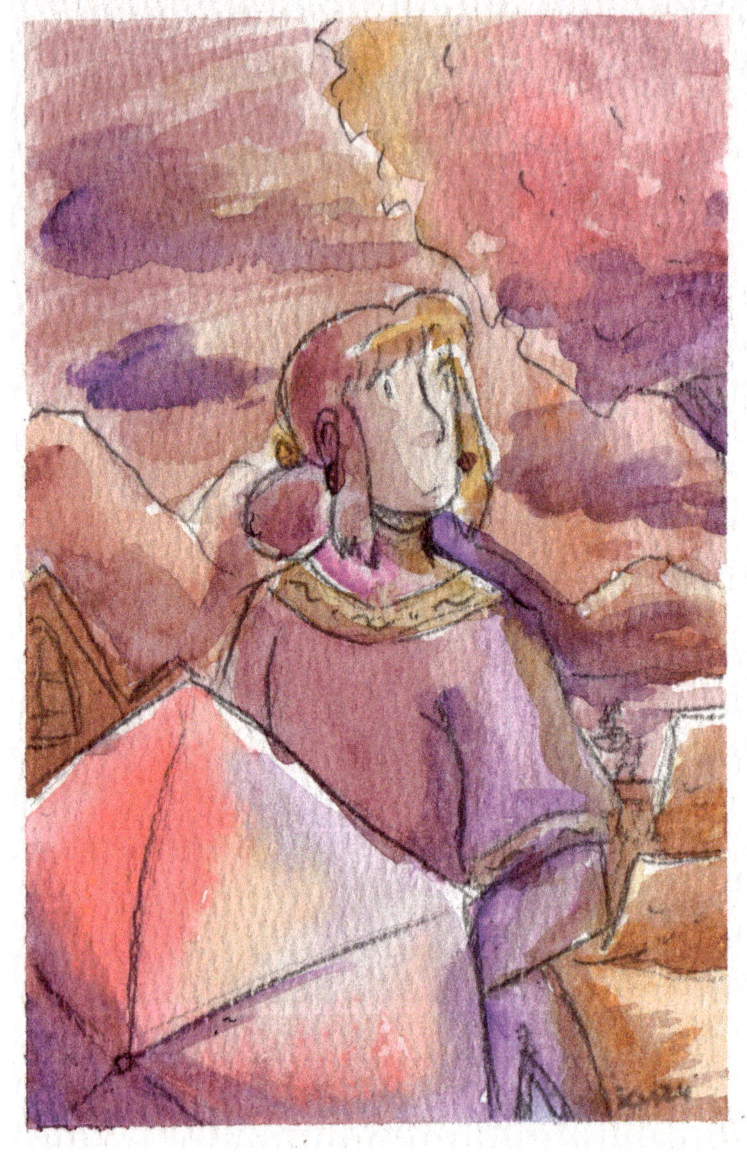

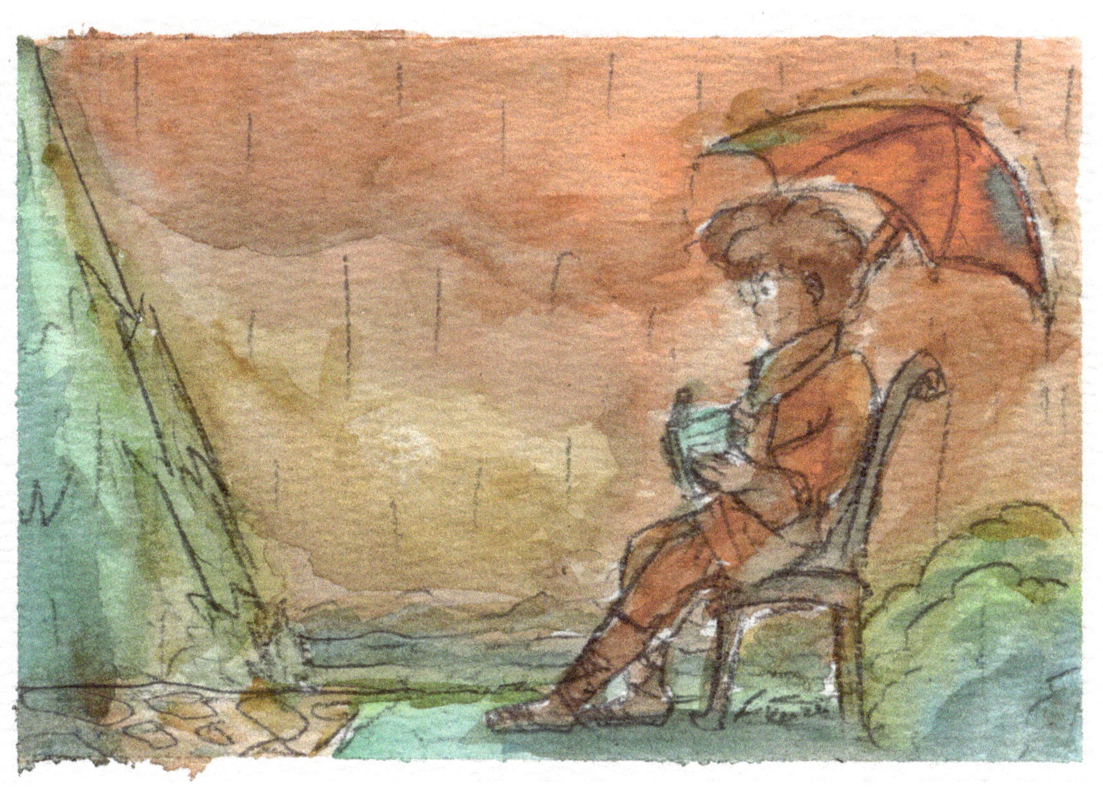

Orange

Yellow

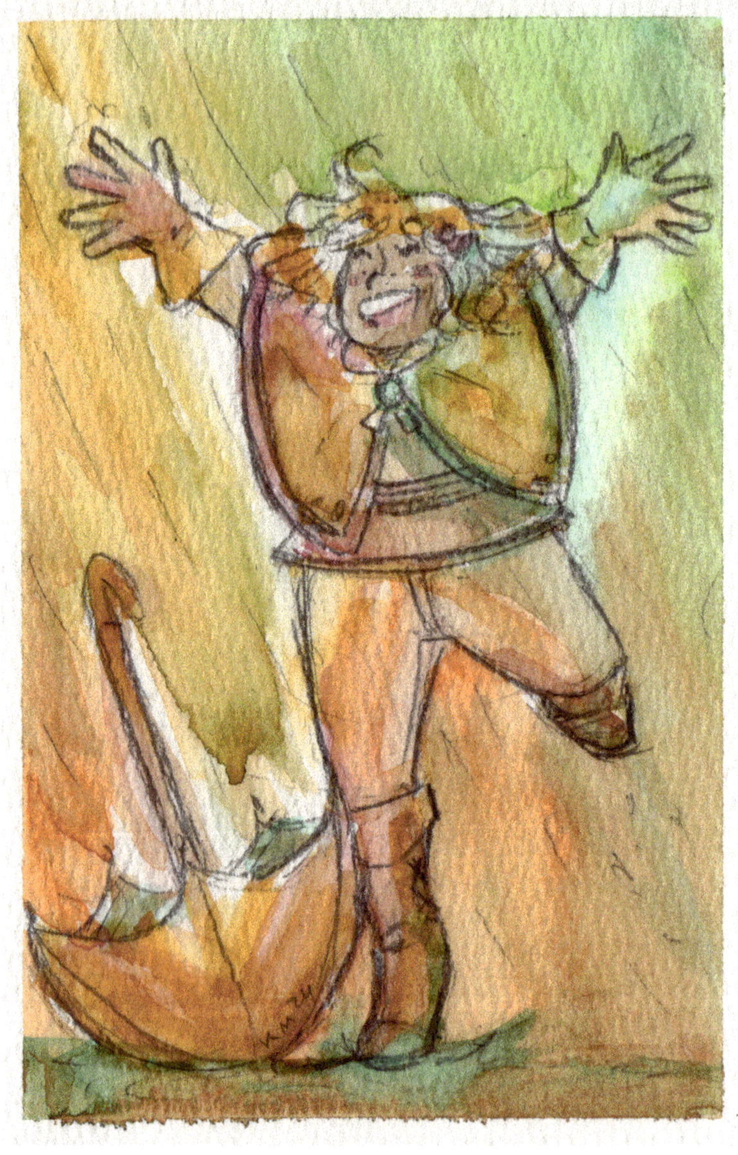

Green

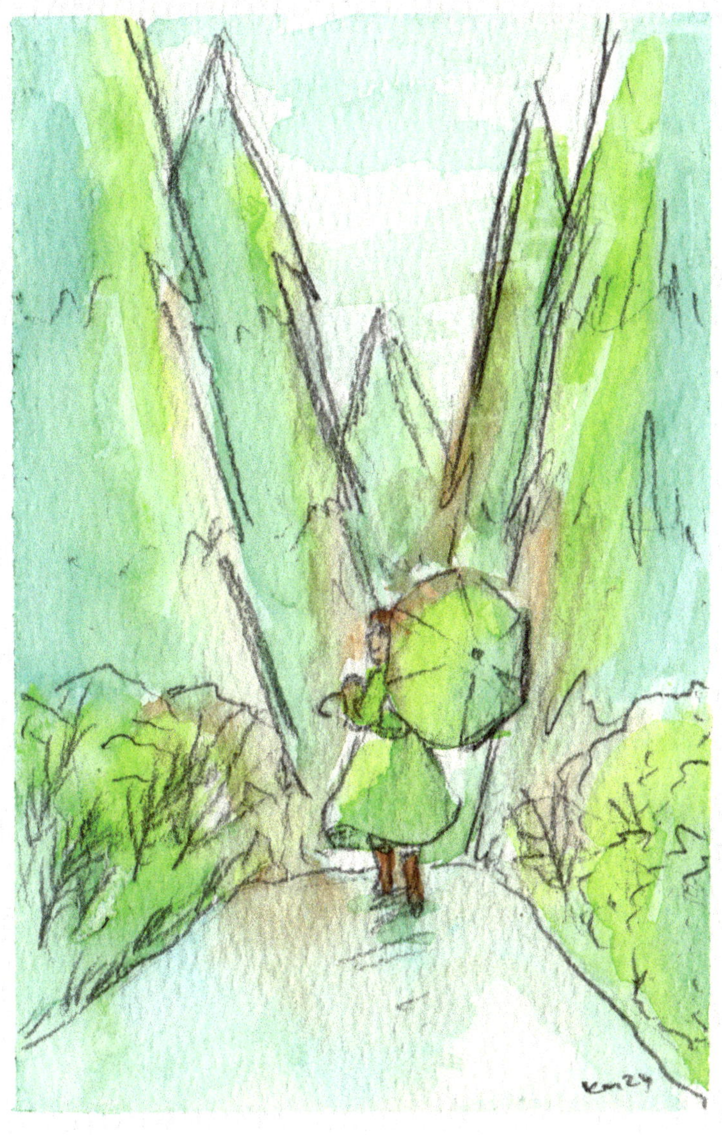

Blue

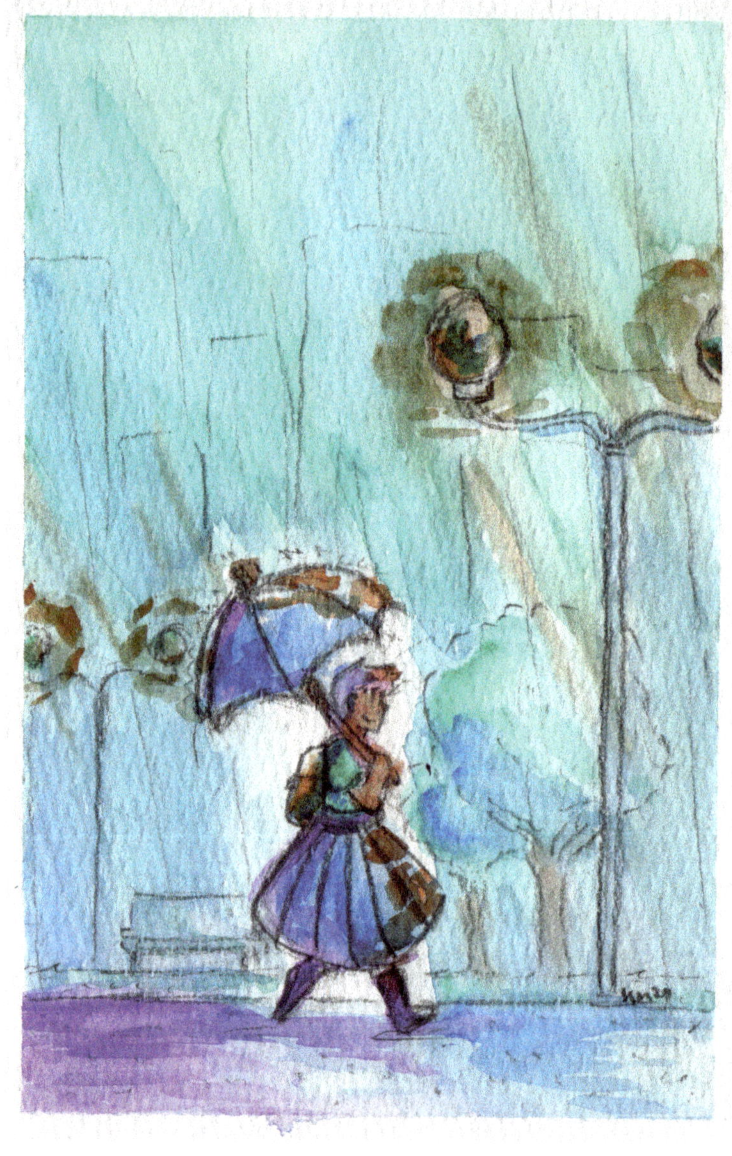

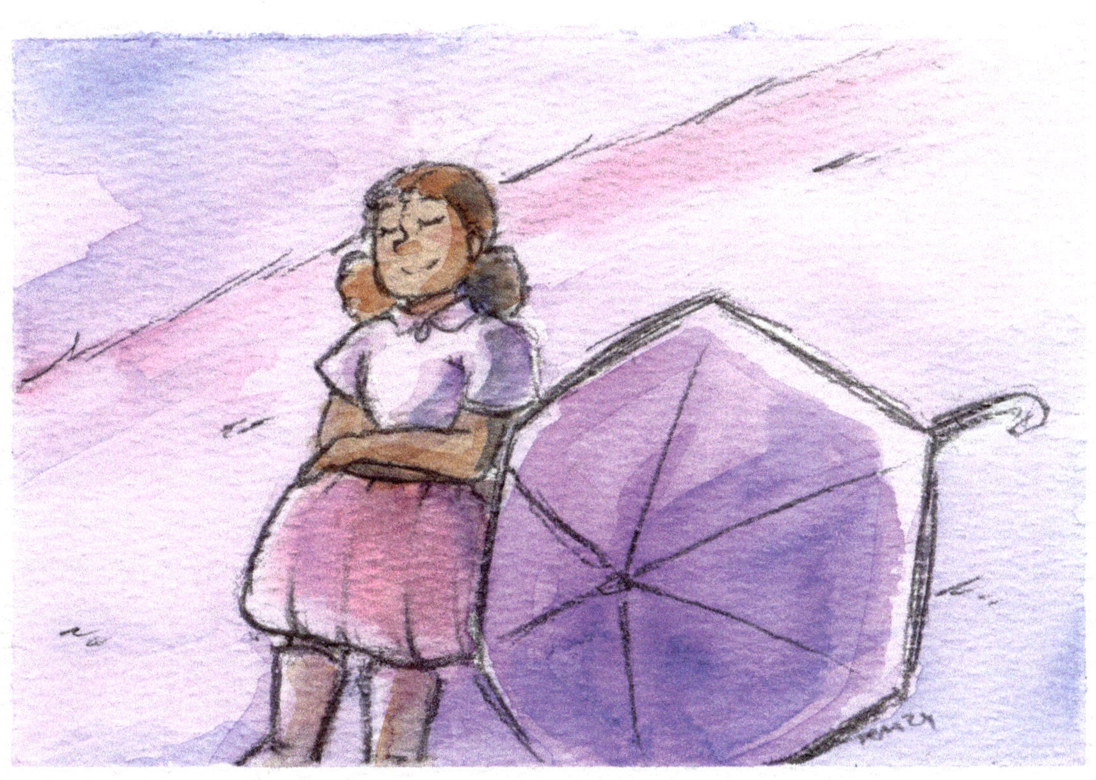

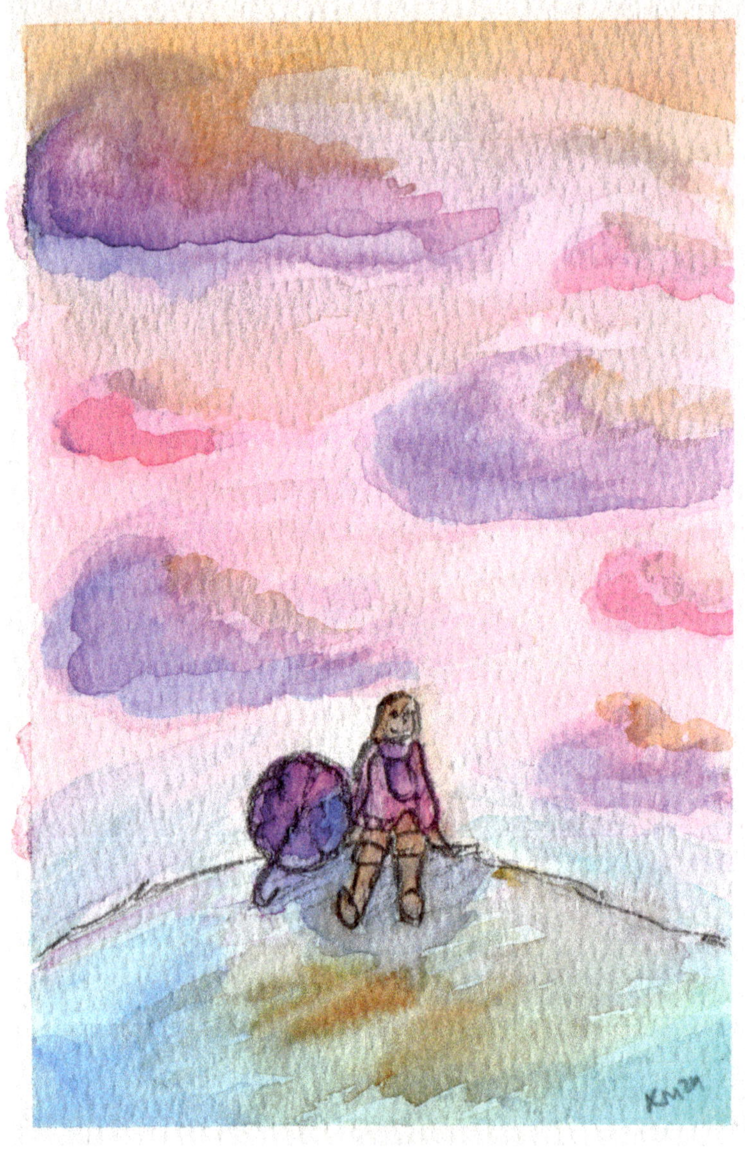

Winter
Fairies

Snowflake

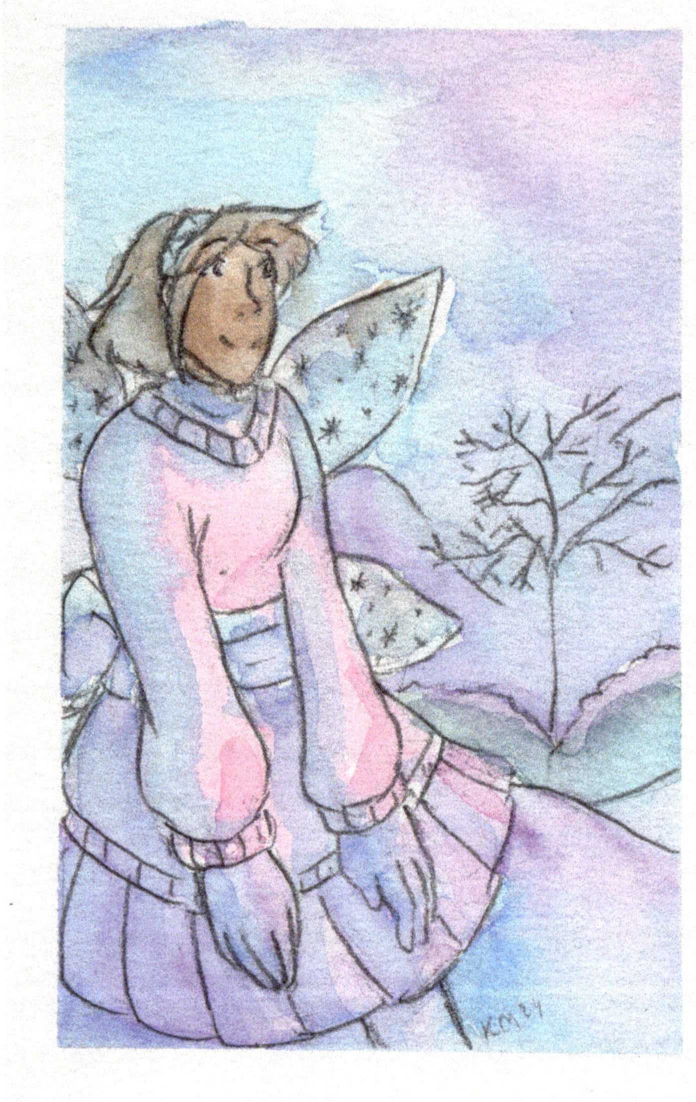

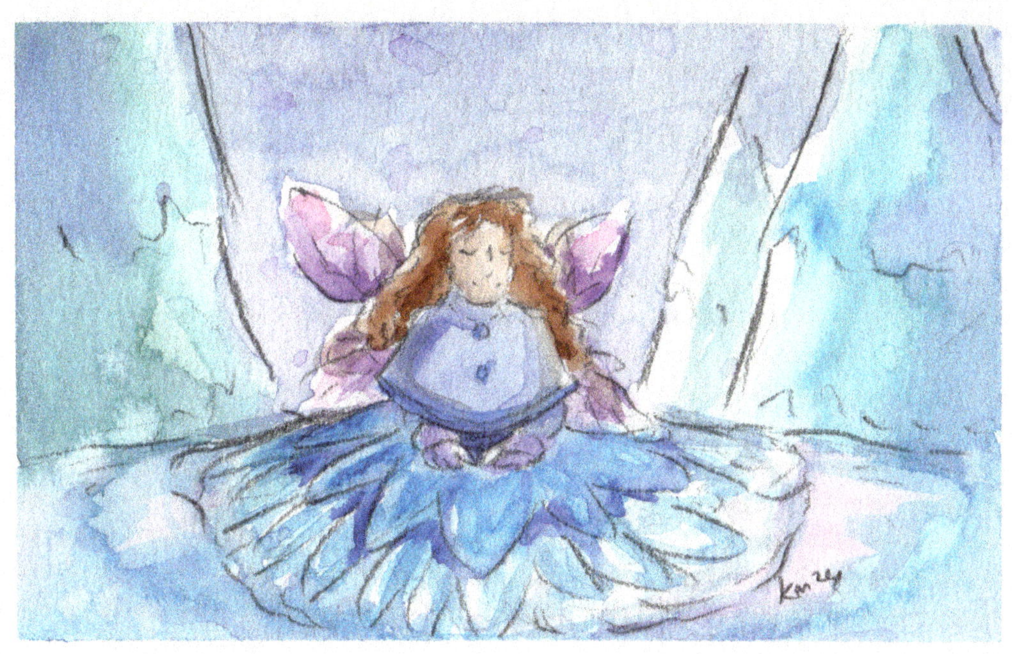

Blizzard

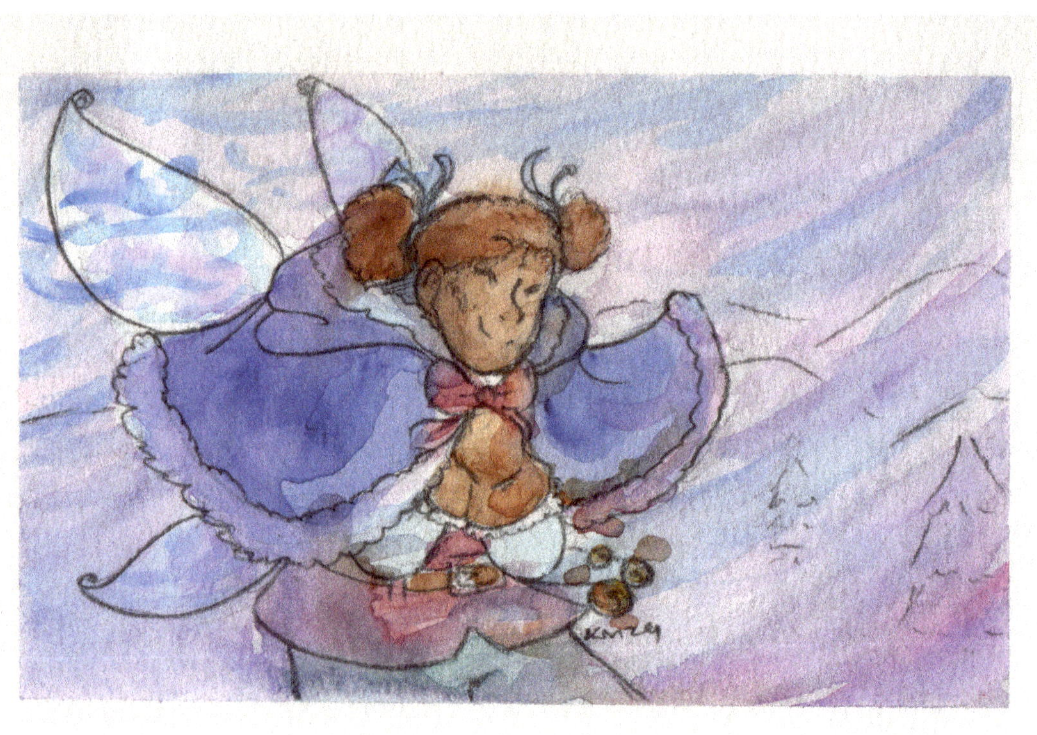

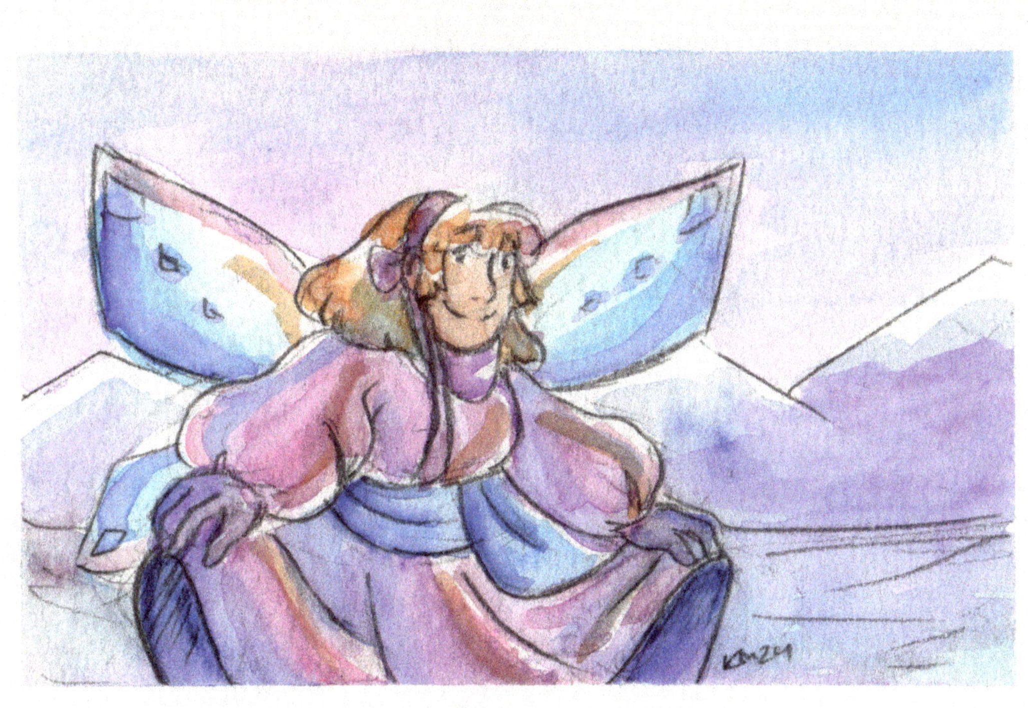

Icicle

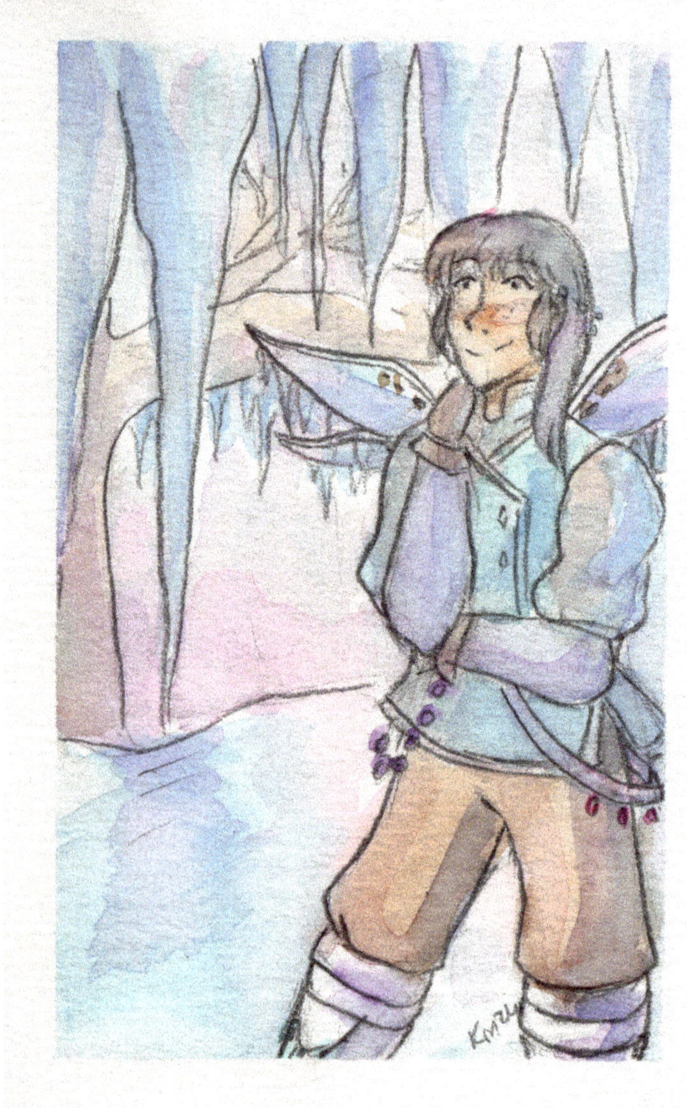

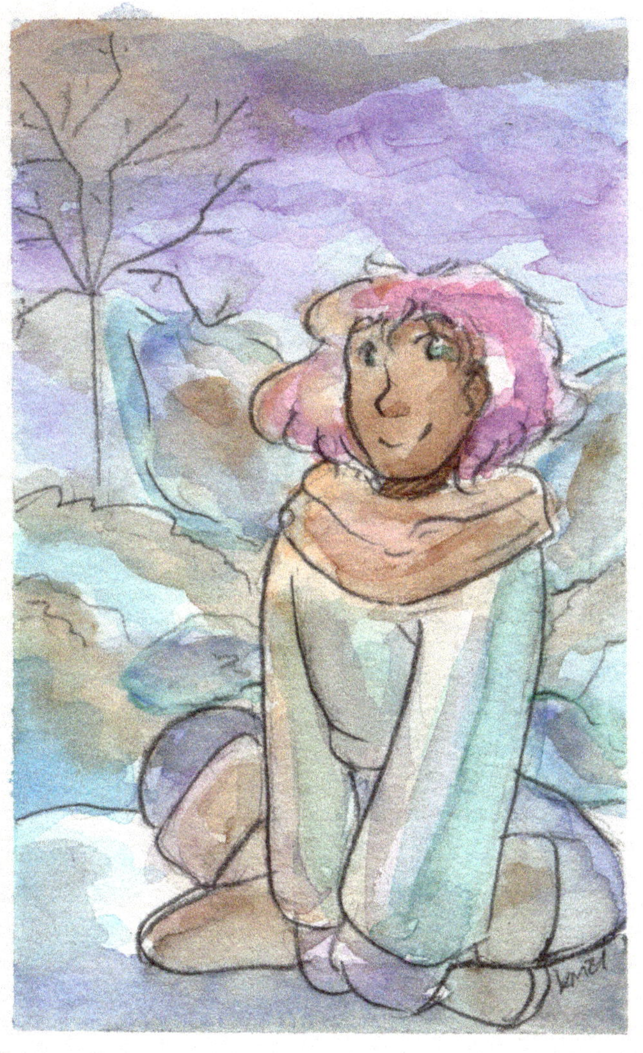

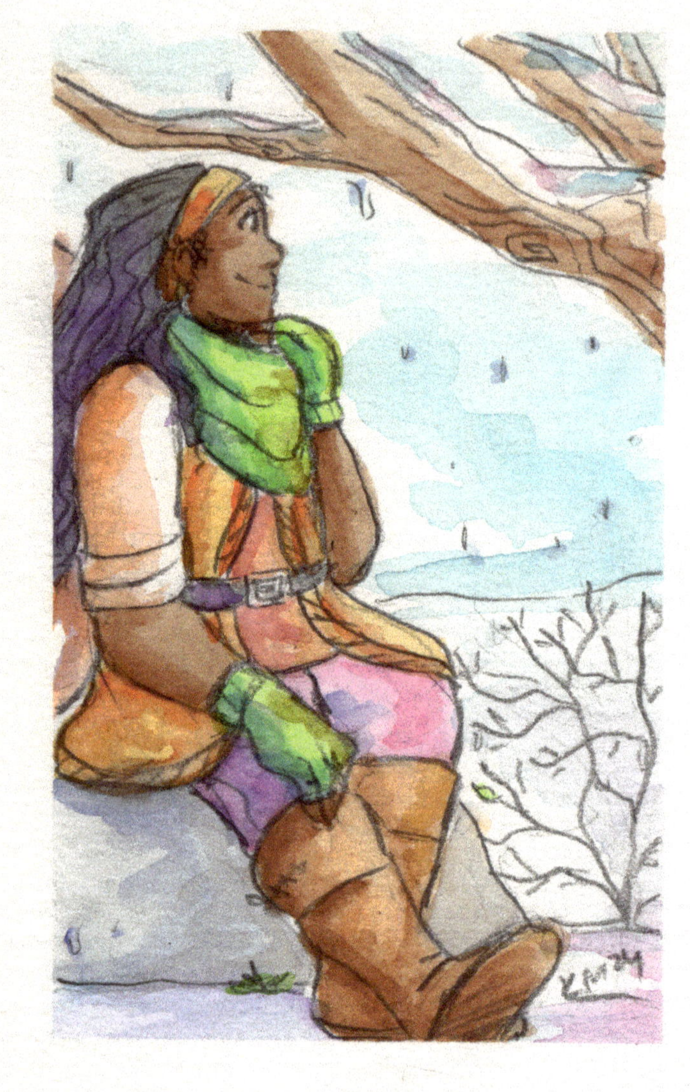

Bees with

Bags

Bumble Bee Tote Bag

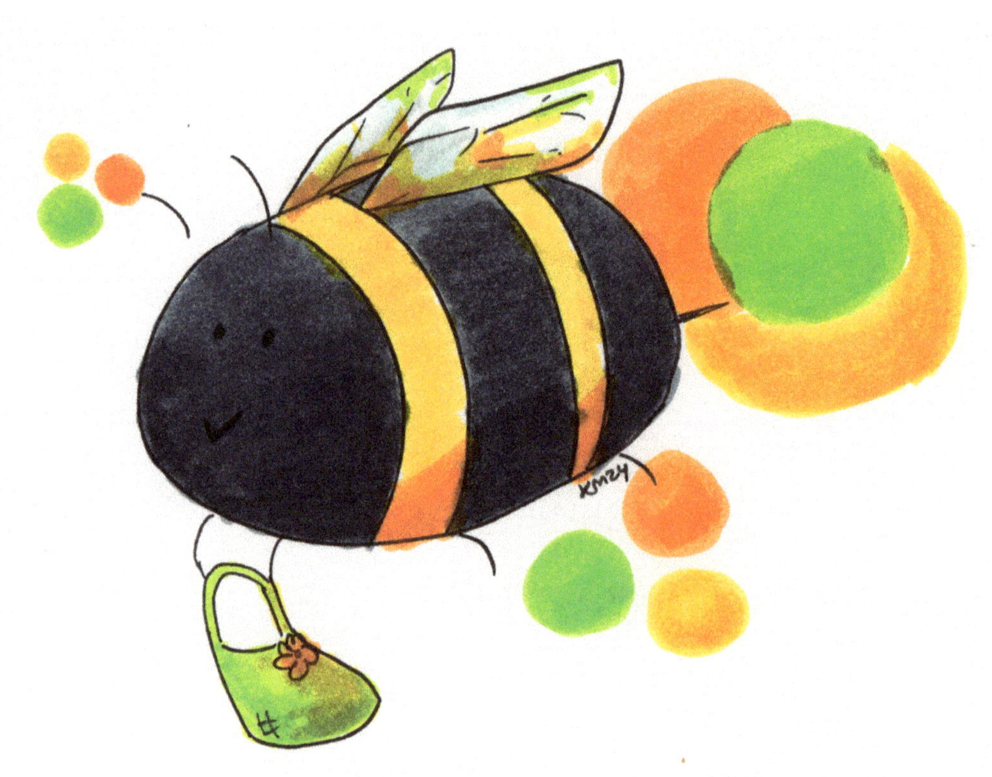

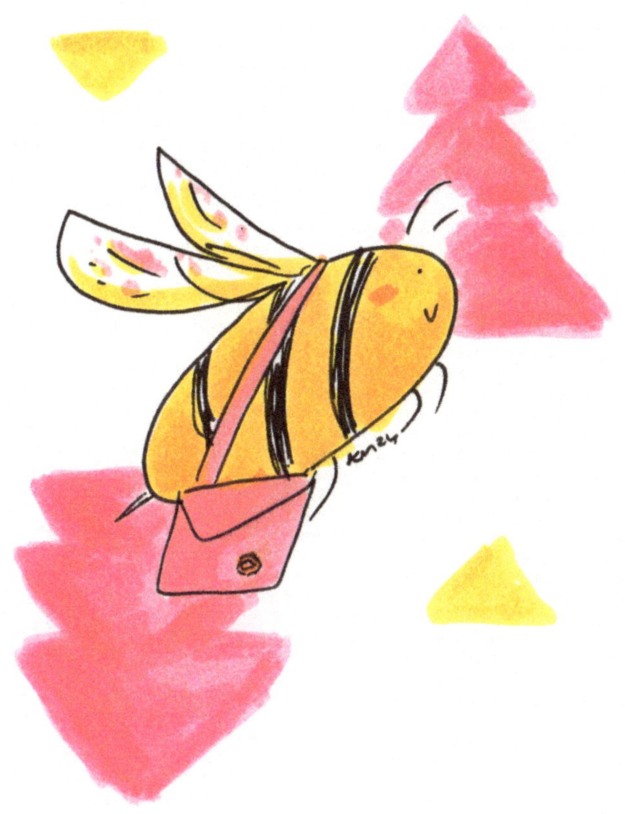

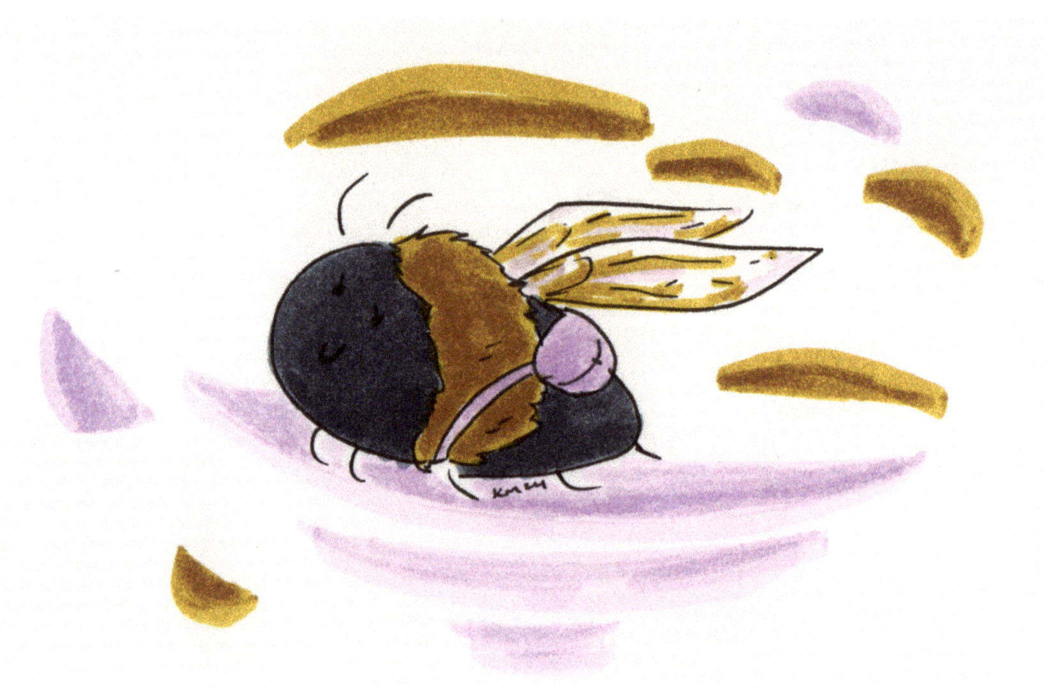

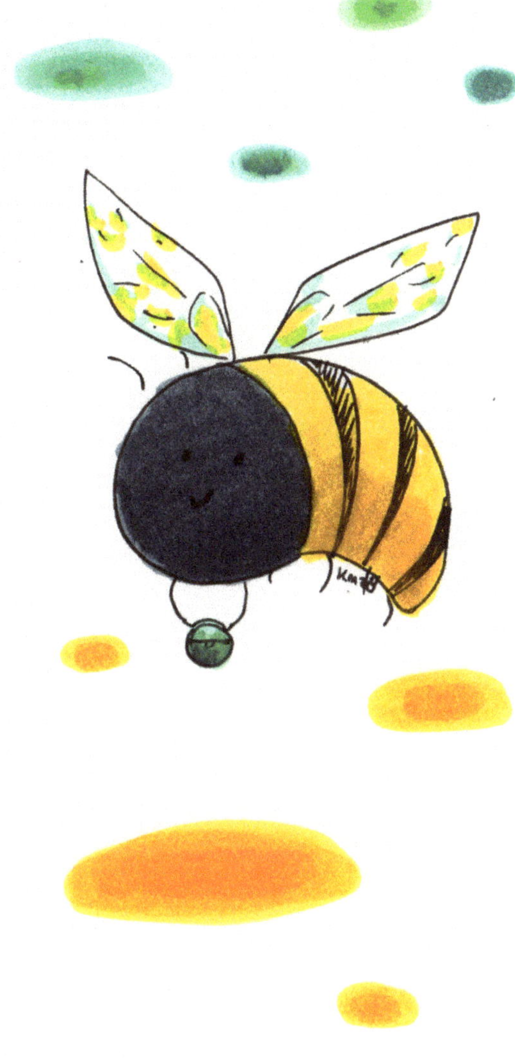

Afterword

Before 2024, I struggled to make single art pieces. I worked with comics and animation and thought better in those formats. Then I had the thought to give each set a theme and started with Flower Fairies. I had fun picking and researching different flowers, making sure to find ones that were distinctive from one another and when I finished the set, I was very happy with how it turned out. For the rest of 2024, I came up with more themes, asking my family for help when I was struggling to think of one. Sometimes I would try a subject that I was unfamiliar with and that I wanted to learn more about, like clouds or different types of cactus (nature really is amazing). It was around Summer when I drew Dino Desserts and Snakes in Hats and they remain two of my favorites. I hope they and the other sets bring joy to you like they have for me! Thank you for looking!

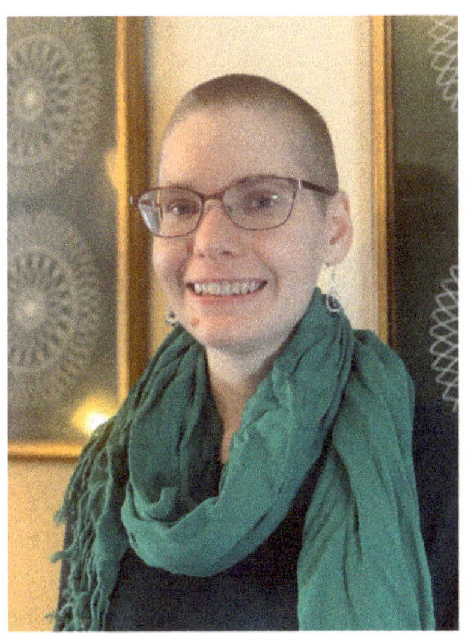

Keilani McConnell is an American artist who enjoys working with color and coming up with fun ideas for illustration series. She has a Bachelor of Music in Flute Performance and both teaches and performs in her local area. She also writes novels, animates, and makes jewelry. To relax, she likes to read, be outside, and play with her kitty, Midna. She works traditionally and her favorite medium is watercolor. She lives in Colorado. For more information, please see her website keilanimcconnellart.com

Cover art © Keilani McConnell 2025
Author photo © Calvin McConnell 2025

www.ingramcontent.com/pod-product-compliance
Lightning Source LLC
Chambersburg PA
CBHW042048030726
47599CB00019B/2404